EUR

Eats, Shoots & Leaves

This Large Print Book carries the
Seal of Approval of N.A.V.H.

Eats, Shoots & Leaves

The Zero Tolerance Approach to Punctuation

Lynne Truss

Thorndike Press • Waterville, Maine

Published in 2004 by arrangement with Gotham Books, a division of Penguin Group (USA) Inc.

Thorndike Press® Large Print Core.

The tree indicium is a trademark of Thorndike Press.

The text of this Large Print edition is unabridged.
Other aspects of the book may vary from the original edition.

Set in 16 pt. Plantin by Minnie B. Raven.

Printed in the United States on permanent paper.

Library of Congress Cataloging-in-Publication Data

Truss, Lynne.
    Eats, shoots & leaves : the zero tolerance approach to punctuation / Lynne Truss.
        p. cm.
    ISBN 0-7862-6837-9 (lg. print : hc : alk. paper)
    1. English language — Punctuation. 2. Large type books.
    I. Title: Eats, shoots, and leaves. II. Title.
    PE1450.T75 2004b
        428.2—dc22   2004051707

To the memory of the striking Bolshevik
printers of St Petersburg who, in 1905,
demanded to be paid the same rate for
punctuation marks as for letters,
and thereby directly precipitated the
first Russian Revolution

As the Founder/CEO of NAVH, the only national health agency solely devoted to those who, although not totally blind, have an eye disease which could lead to serious visual impairment, I am pleased to recognize Thorndike Press★ as one of the leading publishers in the large print field.

Founded in 1954 in San Francisco to prepare large print textbooks for partially seeing children, NAVH became the pioneer and standard setting agency in the preparation of large type.

Today, those publishers who meet our standards carry the prestigious "Seal of Approval" indicating high quality large print. We are delighted that Thorndike Press is one of the publishers whose titles meet these standards. We are also pleased to recognize the significant contribution Thorndike Press is making in this important and growing field.

Lorraine H. Marchi, L.H.D.
Founder/CEO
NAVH

★ Thorndike Press encompasses the following imprints: Thorndike, Wheeler, Walker and Large Print Press.

Contents

Acknowledgements

Thanks are due to the many writers on punctuation who did all the hard work of formulating the clear rules I have doubtless muddied in this book. G. V. Carey's *Mind the Stop* (1939) and Eric Partridge's *You Have a Point There* (1953) are acknowledged classics; modern writers such as David Crystal, Loreto Todd, Graham King, Keith Waterhouse, Tim Austin, Kingsley Amis, Philip Howard, Nicholson Baker, William Hartston and R. L. Trask were all inspirational. Special thanks go to Cathy Stewart, Anne Baker and Gillian Forrester; also to Penny Vine, who set me off on this journey in the first place. Nigel Hall told me the panda joke; Michael Handelzalts told me about the question mark in Hebrew; and Adam Beeson told me where to find the dash on my keyboard. Learned copy-editors have attempted to sort out my commas and save me from embarrassment. I thank them very much. Where faults obstinately remain, they are mine alone. Finally, I would like to thank Andrew Franklin for his encouraging involvement along the way, and the hundreds of readers who generously responded to articles in *The Daily Telegraph*, *The Author* and *Writers' News*. It was very good to know that I was not alone.

Foreword

If Lynne Truss were Catholic I'd nominate her for sainthood. As it is, thousands of English teachers from Maine to Maui will be calling down blessings on her merry, learned head for the gift of her book, *Eats, Shoots & Leaves*.

It's a book about punctuation. Punctuation, if you don't mind! (I hesitated over that exclamation mark, and it's all her doing.) The book is so spirited, so scholarly, those English teachers will sweep all other topics aside to get to, you guessed it, punctuation. Parents and children will gather by the fire many an evening to read passages on the history of the semicolon and the terrible things being done to the apostrophe. Once the poor stepchild of grammar (is that comma OK here?), punctuation will emerge as the Cinderella of the English language.

There are heroes and villains in this book. Oh, you never thought such could be possible? You never thought a book on punctuation could contain raw sex? Well, here is Lynne Truss bemoaning the sad fact she never volunteered to have the babies of Aldus Manutius the Elder (1450–1515). (Help! In that last sentence does the period go inside the parenthesis/ bracket or outside?) If you actually know who Aldus was you get the door prize and, perhaps, Ms. Truss will have your babies.

Aldus Manutius the Elder invented the italic typeface and printed the first semicolon. His son, yes, Aldus the Younger, declared in 1566, "that the main object of punctuation was the clarification of syntax."

"Ho hum," you say or, if you're American, "Big deal." Very well. You're entitled to your ignorance, but pause a moment, dear reader, and imagine this page of deathless prose, the one you're reading, without punctuation.

In the villain department I think greengrocers get a bad rap. No, this doesn't come from Ms. Truss. She merely notes their tendency to stick in apostrophes where apostrophes had never gone before. I feel no such sympathy for the manager of my local supermarket who must have a cellarful of apostrophes he doesn't know what to do with: "Egg's, $1.29 a doz.," for heaven's sake! (In the U.S. it's "heaven's sakes.")

Egg's, and it's not even a possessive.

Lynne Truss has a great soul and I wouldn't mind drinking tea out of a saucer with her — when you read the book you'll see what I mean — except that, on occasion, she lets her Inner Stickler get out of hand. She tells us of "a shopkeeper in Bristol who deliberately stuck ungrammatical signs in his window as a ruse to draw people into the shop; they would come to complain, and he would then talk them into buying something." Then she flings down the gauntlet: ". . . he would be ill-advised to repeat this ploy once my punctuation vigilantes are on the loose." (Notice my masterly use of the ellipsis. Hold your admiration. I owe it all to Lynne.)

I would have that Bristol shopkeeper knighted. Imagine the conversations in his shop. Irate customers skewering him on points of grammar. You could write a play, a movie on this shopkeeper. Track him down, Lynne. Bring him to London. Present him at court.

On second thought, present Lynne Truss at court. The Queen needs cheering up, and what better way than to wax sexy with

Ms. Truss over Aldus Manutius, the Elder and the Younger, their italics, their proto-semicolon.

O, to be an English teacher in the Age of Truss.

— Frank McCourt
January 2004

Publisher's Note

Lynne Truss's *Eats, Shoots &Leaves* has been reprinted exactly as it was in its original British edition, complete with British examples, spellings and, yes, punctuation. There are a few subtle differences between British and American punctuation which the author has addressed in her preface to the North American edition. Any attempt at a complete Americanization of this book would have been akin to an effort to Americanize the Queen of England: futile and, this publisher feels, misguided. Please enjoy this narrative history of punctuation as it was meant to be enjoyed, bone-dry humour and cultural references intact, courtesy of Lynne Truss.

Preface

To be clear from the beginning: no one involved in the production of *Eats, Shoots & Leaves* expected the words "runaway" and "bestseller" would ever be associated with it, let alone upon the cover of an American edition. Had the Spirit of Christmas Bestsellers Yet to Come knocked at the rather modest front door of my small London publisher in the summer of 2003 and said, "I see hundreds of thousands of copies of your little book about punctuation sold before Christmas. It will be debated in every national newspaper and mentioned, yea, even in the House of Lords, where a woman named Lady Strange — I kid thee not — will actually tell the panda joke," I'm afraid the Spirit would have been sent whiffling off down Clerkenwell Road with the sound of merry, disbelieving laughter ringing in its ears. "Lady Strange," we would have repeated, chuckling, for hours afterwards. "Honestly, what are these prophetic spirits of old London town *coming to* these days?"

Personally, I clung on to one thing when

Eats, Shoots & Leaves began its rush up the charts. Since the rallying cry for the book had been chosen pretty early on, I referred to it continually to steady my nerves and remind myself of my original aspirations — which were certainly plucky but at the same time not the least bit confident of universal appeal. "Sticklers unite!" I had written as this rallying cry. "You have nothing to lose but your sense of proportion (and arguably you didn't have a lot of that to begin with)." There you are, then. My hopes for *Eats, Shoots & Leaves* were bold but bathetic; chirpy but feet-on-the-ground; presumptuous yet significantly parenthetical. My book was aimed at the tiny minority of British people "who love punctuation and don't like to see it mucked about with". When my own mother suggested we print on the front of the book "For the select few," I was hurt, I admit it; I bit my lip and blinked a tear. Yet I knew what she meant. I am the writer, after all, who once wrote a whole comic novel about Lewis Carroll and Alfred, Lord Tennyson and expected other people to be interested. Oh yes, I have learned that lesson the hard way.

I still have no idea whether sticklers are uniting in the UK, but I somehow doubt it, despite the staggering sales. Grammatical sticklers are the worst people for finding common cause because it is in their nature (obviously) to pick holes in everyone, even their best friends. Honestly, what an annoying bunch of people. One supporter of *Eats, Shoots & Leaves* wrote a 1,400-word column in *The Times* of London explaining (with glorious self-importance) that while his admiration for my purpose was "total", he disagreed with virtually everything I said. So I am not sure my stickler-chums are, as I write this, sitting down to get things sorted out. What did become depressingly clear, however, was that my personal hunches about the state of the language were horribly correct: standards of punctuation in general in the UK are indeed approaching the point of illiteracy; self-justified philistines ("Get a life!") are truly in the driving seat of our culture; and a lot of well-educated sensitive people really have been weeping friendlessly in caves for the past few years, praying for someone — anyone — to write a book about punctuation with a panda on the cover.

I don't know how bad things are in America, but in the UK I cannot emphasise it enough: standards of punctuation are abysmal. Encouraged to conduct easy tests on television, I discovered to my horror that most British people truly do not know their apostrophe from their elbow. "I'm an Oxbridge intellectual," slurred a chap in Brighton, where we were asking passers-by to "pin the apostrophe on the sentence" for a harmless afternoon chat-show. He immediately placed an apostrophe (oh no!) in a possessive "its". The high-profile editor of a national news-paper made the same mistake on a morning show, scoring two correct points out of a possible seven. On a TV news bulletin, the results of a vox pop item were shown on screen under the heading "Grammar Test" — the spelling of which I assumed was a joke until I realised nobody in the studio was laughing. Meanwhile well-wishers sent hundreds of delightful/horrific examples of idiotic sign-writing, my current favourite being the roadside warning CHILDREN DRIVE SLOWLY — courtesy of the wonderful Shakespearean actor Timothy West. Evidently, this sign — inadvertently descriptive of the dis-appointing road speeds attainable by in-fants at the wheel — was eventually altered (but sadly not improved) by the addition of a comma, becoming CHILDREN, DRIVE

SLOWLY — a kindly exhortation, perhaps, which might even save lives among those self-same reckless juvenile road-users; but still not quite what the writer really had in mind.

By far the oddest and most demoralising response to my book, however, took place at a bookshop event in Piccadilly. It is a story that, if nothing else, proves the truth of that depressing old adage about taking a horse to water. I was signing copies of my book when a rather bedraggled woman came up and said, despairingly, "Oh, I'd *love* to learn about punctuation." Spotting a sure thing (you know how it is), I said with a little laugh, "Then this is the book for you, madam!" I believe my pen actually hovered above the dedication page, as I waited for her to tell me her name.

"No, I mean it," she insisted — as if I had disagreed with her. "I really would *love* to know how to do it. I mean, I did learn it at school, but I've forgotten it now, and it's awful. I put all my commas in the wrong place, and as for the apostrophe . . . !" I nodded, still smiling. This all seemed familiar enough. "So shall I sign it to anyone in particular?" I said. "And I'm a *teacher*," she went on. "And I'm quite ashamed really, not knowing about grammar and all that; so I'd love to know about punctuation, but the trouble is, *there's just nowhere you can turn, is there?*"

This was quite unsettling. She shrugged, defeated, and I hoped she would go away. I said again that the book really did explain many basic things about punctuation; she said again that the basic things of punctuation were *exactly* what nobody was ever prepared to explain to an adult person. I must admit, I started to wonder feverishly whether I was being secretly filmed by publishers of rival punctuation books who had set up the whole thing. I even wondered briefly: had any author in Hatchards (a bookseller established in 1797) ever hit a customer, or was I destined to be the first? Throughout the encounter, I kept smiling at her and nodding at the book, but she never took the hint. In the end, thank goodness, she slid away, leaving me to put my coat over my head and scream.

It was the same kind of strenuous apathy, I suppose, that I refer to on page 58, drawing on the deathless line in Woody Allen's *Small Time Crooks*: "I've always wanted to know how to spell Connecticut." I tend to feel that if a person genuinely wants to know how to spell Connecticut, you see, they will make efforts to look it up. Or, failing that, if a book announcing itself as *The Only Way to Spell Connecticut is This* is to be found in heaps on a table in front of them, they will think, "Hang on, I might get this!" But it turns out there are people whom you simply cannot help, because it suits them to say, with a shrug, "Do you know, I've always wanted to know how to use an apostrophe — and oh dear, I don't know how to wash my hair either." The fact that these people are sometimes editors of national newspapers and Oxbridge intellectuals is just an indication of how low our society's intellectual aspirations have sunk.

It is customary in the UK, incidentally, to blame all examples of language erosion on the pernicious influence of the US. Certainly American spellings are creeping in to our shop signs (GLAMOR GIRL! I noticed in a huge chain pharmacy over Christmas — where it ought to have been "Glamour" with a "u"). But in the case of our deteriorating understanding of commas and apostrophes, we have no one to blame but ourselves. While significant variations exist between British and American usage, these are matters for quite rarefied concern. You say "parentheses" while we say "brackets" (see page 179) — but to people who call an apostrophe "one of them floating comma things" it doesn't matter very much. They are unlikely to spot that American usage interestingly places all terminal punctuation inside closing quotation marks, while British usage sometimes "picks and chooses". (Like that.) People who identify "that dot-thing" as the mark at the end of a sentence probably don't care that the American "period" is the equivalent of the British "full stop", or that "exclamation point" is the US way of saying "exclamation mark". We probably don't use the term "inverted commas" as much as we used to in Britain, but nobody in America has forced us to give them up.

My American correspondents, however, have made it pretty clear that the US is not immune to similar levels of public illiteracy. Carved in stone (in *stone,* mind you) in a Florida shopping mall one may see the splendidly apt quotation from Euripides, "Judge a tree from it's fruit: not the leaves" — and it is all too easy to imagine the stone-mason dithering momentarily over that monumental apostrophe, mallet in hand, chisel poised. Can an apostrophe ever be wrong, he asks himself, as he answers "Nah!" and decisively strikes home and the chips fly out. Meanwhile a casual drive in America is quite as horrifying to a stickler as it is in the UK. CHILDRENS HOME; READERS OUTLET; PLEASE DO NOT LOCK THIS DOOR BETWEEN THE HOUR'S OF 9AM AND 6:30PM.

Might the tide turn, however? Are there any reasons to be cheerful on behalf of punctuation? Well, there is one — and although modesty ought to forbid me from mentioning it, it is the astonishing response *Eats, Shoots & Leaves* has had in the UK. Some may say that the British are obsessed with class difference and that knowing your apostrophes is a way of belittling the uneducated. To which accusation, I say (mainly), "Pah!" How can it be a matter of class difference when ignorance is universal? Why should it only be middle-class people who care about the language? I come personally from a working-class background. I went to a state school, and there are many street traders in my immediate family. Punctuation is no more a class issue than the air we breathe. It is a system of printers' marks that has aided the clarity of the written word for the past half-millennium, and if its time has come to be replaced, let's just use this moment to celebrate what an elegant and imaginative job it did while it had the chance. Caring about matters of language is unfortunately generally associated with small-minded people, but that doesn't make it a small issue. The disappearance of punctuation (including word spacing, capital letters, and so on) indicates an enormous shift in our attitude to the written word, and nobody knows where it will end.

In the meantime, however, I suggest that we ponder the case of Defeatist Bookshop Woman, and consider what she must be like to live with. I may even have to write a fictional character based on her. I can see her now, holding up the queue at an ice-cream vendor, explaining her predicament: "If only one could get an ice cream from somewhere, but it's hopeless!" Or standing outside Lincoln Center with a ticket labelled "Bolshoi" in her hand, saying, "If only I could see a ballet once in my life! But I suppose it's not to be."

Introduction —

The Seventh Sense

Either this will ring bells for you, or it won't. A printed banner has appeared on the concourse of a petrol station near to where I live. "Come inside," it says, "for CD's, VIDEO's, DVD's, and BOOK's."

If this satanic sprinkling of redundant apostrophes causes no little gasp of horror or quickening of the pulse, you should probably put down this book at once. By all means congratulate yourself that you are not a pedant or even a stickler; that you are happily equipped to live in a world of plummeting punctuation standards; but just don't bother to go any further. For any true stickler, you see, the sight of the plural word "Book's" with an apostrophe in it will trigger a ghastly private emotional process similar to the stages of bereavement, though greatly accelerated. First there is shock. Within seconds, shock gives way to disbelief, disbelief to pain, and pain to anger. Finally (and this is where the analogy breaks down), anger gives way to a righteous urge to perpetrate an act of criminal damage with the aid of a permanent marker.

It's tough being a stickler for punctuation these days. One almost dare not get up in the mornings. True, one occasionally hears a marvellous punctuation-fan joke about a panda who "eats, shoots and leaves", but in general the stickler's exquisite sensibilities are assaulted from all sides, causing feelings of panic and isolation. A sign at a health club will announce, "I'ts party time, on Saturday 24th May we are have a disco/party night for free, it will be a ticket only evening." Advertisements offer decorative services to "wall's — ceiling's — door's ect". Meanwhile a newspaper placard announces "FAN'S FURY AT STADIUM INQUIRY", which sounds quite interesting until you look inside the paper and discover that the story concerns a quite large mob of fans, actually — not just the lone hopping-mad fan so promisingly indicated by the punctuation.

Everywhere one looks, there are signs of ignorance and indifference. What about that film *Two Weeks Notice*? Guaranteed to give sticklers a very nasty turn, that was — its posters slung along the sides of buses in letters four feet tall, with no apostrophe in sight. I remember, at the start of the *Two Weeks Notice* publicity campaign in the spring of 2003, emerging cheerfully from Victoria Station (was I whistling?) and stopping dead in my tracks with my fingers in my mouth. Where was the apostrophe? Surely there should be an apostrophe on that bus? If it were "one month's notice" there would be an apostrophe (I reasoned); yes, and if it were "one week's notice" there would be an apostrophe. Therefore "two weeks' notice" requires an apostrophe! Buses that I should have caught (the 73; two 38s) sailed off up Buckingham Palace Road while I communed thus at length with my inner stickler, unable to move or, indeed, regain any sense of perspective.

Part of one's despair, of course, is that the world cares nothing for the little shocks endured by the sensitive stickler. While we look in horror at a badly punctuated sign, the world carries on around us, blind to our plight. We are like the little boy in *The Sixth Sense* who can see dead people, except that we can see dead punctuation. Whisper it in petrified little-boy tones: dead punctuation is invisible to everyone else — yet we see it *all the time*. No one understands us seventh-sense people. They regard us as freaks. When we point out illiterate mistakes we are often aggressively instructed to "get a life" by people who, interestingly, display no evidence of having lives themselves. Naturally we become timid about making our insights known, in such inhospitable conditions. Being burned as a witch is not safely enough off the agenda. A sign has gone up in a local charity-shop window which says, baldly, "Can you spare any old records" (no question mark) and I dither daily outside on the pavement. Should I go in and mention it? It does *matter* that there's no question mark on a direct question. It is appalling ignorance. But what will I do if the elderly charity-shop lady gives me the usual disbelieving stare and then tells me to bugger off, get a life and mind my own business?

On the other hand, I'm well aware there is little profit in asking for sympathy for sticklers. We are not the easiest people to feel sorry for. We refuse to patronise any shop with checkouts for "eight items or less" (because it should be "fewer"), and we got very worked up after 9/11 not because of Osama bin-Laden but because people on the radio kept saying "enormity" when they meant "magnitude", and we really hate that. When we hear the construction "Mr Blair was stood" (instead of "standing") we suck our teeth with annoyance, and when words such as "phenomena", "media" or "cherubim" are treated as singular ("The media says it was quite a phenomena looking at those cherubims"), some of us cannot suppress actual screams. Sticklers never read a book without a pencil at hand, to correct the typographical errors. In short, we are unattractive know-all obsessives who get things out of proportion and are in continual peril of being disowned by our exasperated families.

I know precisely when my own damned stickler personality started to get the better of me. In the autumn of 2002, I was making a series of programmes about punctuation for Radio 4 called *Cutting a Dash*. My producer invited John Richards of the Apostrophe Protection Society to come and talk to us. At that time, I was quite tickled by the idea of an Apostrophe Protection Society, on whose website could be found photographic examples of ungrammatical signs such as "The judges decision is final" and "No dog's". We took Mr Richards on a trip down Berwick Street Market to record his reaction to some greengrocers' punctuation ("Potato's" and so on), and then sat down for a chat about how exactly one goes about protecting a conventional printer's mark that, through no fault of its own, seems to be terminally flailing in a welter of confusion.

What the APS does is write courteous letters, he said. A typical letter would explain the correct use of the apostrophe, and express the gentle wish that, should the offending "BOB,S PETS" sign (with a comma) be replaced one day, this well-meant guidance might be borne in mind. It was at this point that I felt a profound and unignorable stirring. It was the awakening of my Inner Stickler. "But that's not enough!" I said. Suddenly I was a-buzz with ideas. What about issuing stickers printed with the words "This apostrophe is not necessary"? What about telling people to shin up ladders at dead of night with an apostrophe-shaped stencil and a tin of paint? Why did the Apostrophe Protection Society not have a militant wing? Could I start one? Where do you get balaclavas?

,

Punctuation has been defined many ways. Some grammarians use the analogy of stitching: punctuation as the basting that holds the fabric of language in shape. Another writer tells us that punctuation marks are the traffic signals of language: they tell us to slow down, notice this, take a detour, and stop. I have even seen a rather fanciful reference to the full stop and comma as "the invisible servants in fairy tales — the ones who bring glasses of water and pillows, not storms of weather or love". But best of all, I think, is the simple advice given by the style book of a national newspaper: that punctuation is "a courtesy designed to help readers to understand a story without stumbling".

Isn't the analogy with good manners perfect? Truly good manners are invisible: they ease the way for others, without drawing attention to themselves. It is no accident that the word "punctilious" ("attentive to formality or etiquette") comes from the same original root word as punctuation. As we shall see, the practice of "pointing" our writing has always been offered in a spirit of helpfulness, to underline meaning and prevent awkward misunderstandings between writer and reader. In 1644 a schoolmaster from Southwark, Richard Hodges, wrote in his *The English Primrose* that "great care ought to be had in writing, for the due observing of points: for, the neglect thereof will pervert the sense", and he quoted as an example, "My Son, if sinners intise [entice] thee consent thou, not refraining thy foot from their way." Imagine the difference to the sense, he says, if you place the comma after the word "not": "My Son, if sinners intise thee consent thou not, refraining thy foot from their way." This was the 1644 equivalent of Ronnie Barker in *Porridge*, reading the sign-off from a fellow lag's letter from home, "Now I must go and get on my lover", and then pretending to notice a comma, so hastily changing it to, "Now I must go and get on, my lover."

To be fair, many people who couldn't punctuate their way out of a paper bag are still interested in the way punctuation can alter the sense of a string of words. It is the basis of all "I'm sorry, I'll read that again" jokes. Instead of "What would you with the king?" you can have someone say in Marlowe's *Edward II*, "What? Would you? *With the king?*" The consequences of mispunctuation (and re-punctuation) have appealed to both great and little minds, and in the age of the fancy-that email a popular example is the comparison of two sentences:

A woman, without her man, is nothing.
A woman: without her, man is nothing.

Which, I don't know, really makes you *think*, doesn't it? Here is a popular "Dear Jack" letter that works in much the same fundamentally pointless way:

Dear Jack,

I want a man who knows what love is all about. You are generous, kind, thoughtful. People who are not like you admit to being useless and inferior. You have ruined me for other men. I yearn for you. I have no feelings whatsoever when we're apart. I can be forever happy — will you let me be yours?

Jill

Dear Jack,

I want a man who knows what love is. All about you are generous, kind, thoughtful people, who are not like you. Admit to being useless and inferior. You have ruined me. For other men I yearn! For you I have no feelings whatsoever. When we're apart I can be forever happy. Will you let me be?

Yours,
Jill

35

But just to show there is nothing very original about all this, five hundred years before email a similarly tiresome puzzle was going round:

Every Lady in this Land
Hath 20 Nails on *each* Hand;
Five & twenty on Hands *and Feet*;
And this is true, without deceit.

(Every lady in this land has twenty nails. On each hand, five; and twenty on hands and feet.)

So all this is quite amusing, but it is noticeable that no one emails the far more interesting example of the fateful mispunctuated telegram that precipitated the Jameson Raid on the Transvaal in 1896 — I suppose that's a reflection of modern education for you. Do you know of the Jameson Raid, described as a "fiasco"? Marvellous punctuation story. Throw another log on that fire. The Transvaal was a Boer republic at the time, and it was believed that the British and other settlers around Johannesburg (who were denied civil rights) would rise up if Jameson invaded. But unfortunately, when the settlers sent their telegraphic invitation to Jameson, it included a tragic ambiguity:

It is under these circumstances that we feel constrained to call upon you to come to our aid should a disturbance arise here the circumstances are so extreme that we cannot but believe that you and the men under you will not fail to come to the rescue of people who are so situated.

As Eric Partridge points out in his *Usage and Abusage*, if you place a full stop after the word "aid" in this passage, the message is unequivocal. It says, "Come at once!" If you put it after "here", however, it says something more like, "We might need you at some later date depending on what happens here, but in the meantime — don't call us, Jameson, old boy; we'll call you." Of course, the message turned up at *The Times* with a full stop after "aid" (no one knows who put it there) and poor old Jameson just sprang to the saddle, without anybody wanting or expecting him to.

All of which substantiates Partridge's own metaphor for punctuation, which is that it's "the line along which the train (composition, style, writing) must travel if it isn't to run away with its driver". In other words, punctuation keeps sense on the rails. Of course people will always argue over levels of punctuation, accusing texts of having too much or too little. There is an enjoyable episode in Peter Hall's *Diaries* when, in advance of directing Albert Finney in *Hamlet,* he "fillets" the text of "practically all its punctuation except what is essential to sense" and then finds he has to live with the consequences. On August 21, 1975, he notes, "Shakespeare's text is always absurdly over-punctuated; generations of scholars have tried to turn him into a good grammarian." All of which sounds sensible enough, until we find the entry for the first rehearsal on September 22, which he describes as "good" but also admits was "a rough and ready, stumbling reading, with people falling over words or misplaced emphases".

,

What happened to punctuation? Why is it so disregarded when it is self-evidently so useful in preventing enormous mix-ups? A headline in today's paper says, "DEAD SONS PHOTOS MAY BE RELEASED" — the story relating to dead sons in the plural, but you would never know. The obvious culprit is the recent history of education practice. We can blame the pedagogues. Until 1960, punctuation was routinely taught in British schools. A child sitting a County Schools exam in 1937 would be asked to punctuate the following puzzler: "Charles the First walked and talked half an hour after his head was cut off" (answer: "Charles the First walked and talked. Half an hour after, his head was cut off"). Today, thank goodness, the National Curriculum ensures that when children are eight, they are drilled in the use of the comma, even if their understanding of grammar is at such an early age a bit hazy. For *Cutting a Dash* we visited a school in Cheshire where quite small children were being taught that you use commas in the following situations:

1 in a list
2 before dialogue
3 to mark out additional information

Which was very impressive. Identifying "additional information" at the age of eight is quite an achievement, and I know for a fact that I couldn't have done it. But if things are looking faintly more optimistic under the National Curriculum, there remains the awful truth that, for over a quarter of a century, punctuation and English grammar were simply not taught in the majority of schools, with the effect that A-level examiners annually bewailed the condition of examinees' written English, while nothing was done. Candidates couldn't even *spell* the words "grammar" and "sentence", let alone use them in any well-informed way.

Attending a grammar school myself between 1966 and 1973, I don't remember being taught punctuation, either. There was a comical moment in the fifth year when our English teacher demanded, "But you *have* had lessons in grammar?" and we all looked shifty, as if the fault was ours. We had been taught Latin, French and German grammar; but English grammar was something we felt we were expected to infer from our reading — which is doubtless why I came a cropper over "its" and "it's". Like many uninstructed people, I surmised that, if there was a version of "its" with an apostrophe *before* the "s", there was somehow logically bound to be a version of "its" with an apostrophe *after* the "s" as well. A shame no one set me right on this common misapprehension, really. But there you are. I just remember a period when, convinced that an apostrophe was definitely required *somewhere*, I would cunningly suspend a very small one immediately above the "s", to cover all eventualities. Imagine my teenage wrath when, time after time, my homework was returned with this well-meant floating apostrophe struck out. "Why?" I would rail, using all my powers of schoolgirl inference and getting nowhere. Hadn't I balanced it perfectly? How could the teacher possibly tell I had put it in the wrong place?

Luckily for me, I was exceptionally interested in English and got there in the end. While other girls were out with boyfriends on Sunday afternoons, getting their necks disfigured by love bites, I was at home with the wireless listening to an Ian Messiter quiz called *Many a Slip*, in which erudite and amusing contestants spotted grammatical errors in pieces of prose. It was a fantastic programme. I dream sometimes they have brought it back. Panellists such as Isobel Barnett and David Nixon would interrupt Roy Plomley with a *buzz* and say "Tautology!" Around this same time, when other girls of my age were attending the Isle of Wight Festival and having abortions, I bought a copy of Eric Partridge's *Usage and Abusage* and covered it in sticky-backed plastic so that it would last a lifetime (it has). Funny how I didn't think any of this was peculiar at the time, when it was behaviour with "Proto Stickler" written all over it. But I do see now why it was no accident that I later wound up as a sub-editor with a literal blue pencil.

But to get back to those dark-side-of-the-moon years in British education when teachers upheld the view that grammar and spelling got in the way of self-expression, it is arguable that the timing of their grammatical apathy could not have been worse. In the 1970s, no educationist would have predicted the explosion in universal written communication caused by the personal computer, the internet and the key-pad of the mobile phone. But now, look what's happened: everyone's a writer! Everyone is posting film reviews on Amazon that go like this:

I watched this film [*About a Boy*] a few days ago expecting the usual hugh Grant bumbling . . . character I've come to loathe/expect over the years. I was thoroughly suprised. This film was great, one of the best films i have seen in a long time. The film focuses around one man who starts going to a single parents meeting, to meet women, one problem He doesnt have a child.

Isn't this sad? People who have been taught nothing about their own language are (contrary to educational expectations) spending all their leisure hours attempting to string sentences together for the edification of others. And there is no editing on the internet! Meanwhile, in the world of text messages, ignorance of grammar and punctuation obviously doesn't affect a person's ability to communicate messages such as "C U later". But if you try anything longer, it always seems to turn out much like the writing of the infant Pip in *Great Expectations*:

MI DEER JO I OPE U R KRWITE WELL I OPE I SHAL SON B HABELL 4 2 TEEDGE U JO AN THEN WE SHORL B SO GLODD AN WEN I M PRENGTD 2 U JO WOT LARX AN BLEVE ME INF XN PIP.

Now, there are many people who claim that they do fully punctuate text messages. For *Cutting a Dash*, we asked people in the street (outside the Palladium Theatre, as it happens, at about 5pm) if they used proper punctuation when sending text messages, and were surprised — not to say incredulous — when nine out of ten people said yes. Some of them said they used semicolons and parentheses and everything. "I'm a grammar geek," explained one young New Zealand woman. "I'm trying to teach my teenage son to punctuate properly," said a nice scholarly-looking man. I kept offering these respondents an easy way out: "It's a real fag, going through that punctuation menu, though? I mean, it would be quite understandable if you couldn't be bothered." But we had evidently stumbled into Grammar Geek Alley, and there was nothing we could do. "Of course I punctuate my text messages, I did A-level English," one young man explained, with a look of scorn. Evidently an A level in English is a sacred trust, like something out of *The Lord of the Rings*. You must go forth with your A level and protect the English language with your bow of elfin gold.

But do you know what? I didn't believe those people. Either they were weirdly self-selecting or they were simply lying for the microphone. Point out to the newsagent that "DEAD SONS PHOTOS MAY BE RELEASED" is not grammatically complete and he will hastily change the subject to the price of milk. Stand outside a

Leicester Square cinema indicating — with a cut-out apostrophe on a stick — how the title *Two Weeks Notice* might be easily grammatically corrected (I did this), and not a soul will take your side or indeed have a clue what your problem is. And that's sad. Taking our previous analogies for punctuation, what happens when it isn't used? Well, if punctuation is the stitching of language, language comes apart, obviously, and all the buttons fall off. If punctuation provides the traffic signals, words bang into each other and everyone ends up in Minehead. If one can bear for a moment to think of punctuation marks as those invisibly beneficent fairies (I'm sorry), our poor deprived language goes parched and pillowless to bed. And if you take the courtesy analogy, a sentence no longer holds the door open for you to walk in, but drops it in your face as you approach.

The reason it's worth standing up for punctuation is not that it's an arbitrary system of notation known only to an over-sensitive elite who have attacks of the vapours when they see it misapplied. The reason to stand up for punctuation is that without it there is no reliable way of communicating meaning. Punctuation herds words together, keeps others apart. Punctuation directs you how to read, in the way musical notation directs a musician how to play. As we shall see in the chapter on commas, it was first used by Greek dramatists two thousand years ago to guide actors between breathing points — thus leading to the modern explanation of why a cat is not a comma:

A cat has claws at the ends of its paws.
A comma's a pause at the end of a clause.

Words strung together without punctuation recall those murky murals Rolf Harris used to paint, where you kept tilting your head and wondering what it was. Then Rolf would dip a small brush into a pot of white and — to the deathless, teasing line, "Can you guess what it is yet?" — add a line here, a dot there, a curly bit, and suddenly all was clear. Good heavens, it looked like just a splodge of colours and all along it was a kangaroo in football boots having a sandwich! Similarly, take a bit of unpunctuated prose, add the dots and flourishes in the right place, stand back, and what have you got?

My dear Joe,
    I hope you are quite well. I hope I

shall soon be able to teach you, Joe —
and then we shall be so glad. And when
I am apprenticed to you, Joe: *what
larks!* Believe me, in affection,

Pip

,

Every language expert from Dr Johnson
onwards has accepted that it's a mistake to
attempt to "embalm the language". Of
course it must change and adapt. When
the time comes that Pip's original text is
equally readable with the one above, then
our punctuation system can be declared
dead and no one will mind. In the chapters
that follow, we will see how it is in the nature of printers' conventions (which is all
punctuation marks are) to develop over
time, usually in the cause of making language less fussy on the page. It is useful to
remember, however — as we struggle to
preserve a system under attack — that a
reader from a couple of hundred years ago
would be shocked by present-day punctuation that we now regard as flawless and elegant. Why don't we use capital letters for
all nouns any more? Why don't we use full
stops after everyday abbreviations? Why
not combine colons with dashes sometimes? Where did all the commas go? Why

isn't there a hyphen in "today"? Lawks-a-mussy, what sort of punctuation chickens are we at the beginning of the 21st century?

Well, taking just the initial capital letters and the terminating full stop (the rest will come later), they have not always been there. The initial letter of a sentence was first capitalised in the 13th century, but the rule was not consistently applied until the 16th. In manuscripts of the 4th to 7th centuries, the first letter of the page was decorated, regardless of whether it was the start of a sentence — and indeed, while we are on the subject of decorated letters, who can forget the scene in *Not the Nine O'Clock News* in which an elderly, exhausted monk unbent himself after years of illuminating the first page of the Bible, only to see that he had written, gloriously, "Benesis"? Nowadays, the convention for starting a new sentence with a capital letter is so ingrained that word-processing software will not allow you to type a full stop and then a lower case letter; it will capitalise automatically. This is bad news, obviously, for chaps like e.e. cummings, but good news for those who have spotted the inexorable advance of lower case into book titles, television captions, company names and (of course) everything on the non-case-sensitive internet, and lie awake at night worrying about the confusion this is spreading in young minds.

Meanwhile, the full stop is surely the simplest mark to understand — so long as everyone continues to have some idea what a sentence is, which is a condition that can't be guaranteed. As the original "point" (so called by Chaucer), it appears to occupy a place in our grammar that is unassailable. Every time the sentence ends, there is a full stop (or a full-stop substitute such as the exclamation mark or the question mark). As easy as that. If you resort to full stops all the time, by the way, and don't use anything else, and keep to very short sentences, people who have read H. W. Fowler's *The King's English* (1906) will accuse you of "spot plague" and perhaps also assume you are modelling yourself on Ernest Hemingway, but the good news is you can't go wrong grammatically. The American name "period", incidentally, was one of its original English names too. Just as the word "comma" originally referred to the piece of writing itself (rather than the mark that contained it), so "period" referred to a longer piece of writing. Shakespeare called the full stop a period in *A Mid-summer Night's Dream* when he described nervous players "making periods in the midst of sentences". This was on the occasion of one of the first (and unfunniest) scenes of someone wrecking the sense of a speech by putting the full stops in the wrong place:

We do not come as minding to content you,
    Our true intent is. All for your delight
We are not here.
        William Shakespeare,
        A Midsummer Night's Dream,
        Act V, scene i

Ho hum. But we should not be complacent even on behalf of the robust and unambiguous full stop. Young people call them dots, you know. They are now accustomed to following a full stop with a lowercase letter and *no space*. Ask them to write "seven-thirty" in figures (7.30) and they will probably either put a colon in it (because their American software uses a colon for 7:30) or write 7-30 or 7'30. Meanwhile, the illiterate default punctuation mark is nowadays the comma, which gives even more cause for alarm:

The tap water is safe to drink in tea and coffee, however, we recommend using bottled water for drinking, it can be purchased very cheaply in the nearby shops.

Sixty years ago, when he wrote *Mind the Stop*, G. V. Carey gave just one paragraph to the apostrophe, because there was so little to say about it. "If only all marks were so easy," he sighed. But this was in an age when people had been taught the difference between "Am I looking at my dinner or the dog's?" and "Am I looking at my dinner or the dogs?" What I hope will become clear from this book is that one can usefully combine a descriptive and prescriptive approach to what is happening to this single aspect of the language. The descriptive sort of linguist tends to observe change in the language, note it, analyse it and manage not to wake up screaming every night. He will opine that if (say) the apostrophe is turning up in words such as "Books", then that's a sure sign nobody knows how to use it any more; that it has outlasted its usefulness; it is like Tinkerbell with her little light fading, sustained only by elicited applause; it will ultimately fade, extinguish and die. This is a highly sane and healthy point of view, of course — if a little emotionally cool. Meanwhile, at the other end of the spectrum, severely prescriptive grammarians would argue that, since they were taught at school in 1943 that you must never start a sentence with "And" or "But", the modern world is benighted by ignorance and folly, and most of modern literature should be burned.

Somewhere between these positions is where I want us to end up: staunch because we understand the advantages of being staunch; flexible because we understand the rational and historical necessity to be flexible. In *Mind the Stop* Carey defines punctuation as being governed "two-thirds by rule and one-third by personal taste". My own position is simple: in some matters of punctuation there are simple rights and wrongs; in others, one must apply a good ear to good sense. I want the greatest clarity from punctuation, which means, supremely, that I want apostrophes where they should be, and I will not cease from mental fight nor shall my sword sleep in my hand (hang on, didn't "Jerusalem" begin with an "And"?) until everyone knows the difference between "its" and "it's" and bloody well nobody writes about "dead sons photos" without indicating whether the photos in question show one son or several. There is a rumour that in parts of the Civil Service workers have been pragmatically instructed to omit apostrophes because no one knows how to use them any more — and this is the kind of pragmatism, I say along with Winston Churchill, "up with which we shall not put". How dare anyone make this decision on behalf of the apostrophe? What gives the Civil Service — or, indeed, Warner Brothers — the right to decide our Tinkerbell should die? How long will it be before a mainstream publisher allows an illiterate title into print? How long before the last few punctuation sticklers are obliged to take refuge together in caves?

So what I propose is action. Sticklers unite, you have nothing to lose but your sense of proportion, and arguably you didn't have a lot of that to begin with. Maybe we won't change the world, but at least we'll feel better. The important thing is to unleash your Inner Stickler, while at the same time not getting punched on the nose, or arrested for damage to private property. You know the campaign called "Pipe Down", against the use of piped music? Well, ours will be "Pipe Up". Be a nuisance. Do something. And if possible use a bright red pen. Send back emails that are badly punctuated; return letters; picket Harrods. Who cares if members of your family abhor your Inner Stickler and devoutly wish you had an Inner Scooby-Doo instead? At least if you adopt a zero tolerance approach, when you next see a banner advertising "CD's, DVD's, Video's, and Book's", you won't just stay indoors getting depressed about it. Instead you will engage in some direct-action argy-bargy! Because — here's the important thing — you won't be alone.

That's always been the problem for sticklers, you see. The feeling of isolation. The feeling of nerdishness. One solitary obsessive, feebly armed with an apostrophe on a stick, will never have the nerve to demonstrate outside Warner Brothers on the issue of *Two Weeks Notice*. But if enough people could pull together in a common cause, who knows what we might accomplish? There are many obstacles to overcome here, not least our national characteristics of reserve (it's impolite to tell someone they're wrong), apathy (someone else will do it) and outright cowardice (is it worth being duffed up for the sake of a terminally ailing printer's convention?). But I have faith. I do have faith. And I also have

an Inner Stickler that, having been un-
leashed, is now roaring, salivating and
clawing the air in a quite alarming manner.

,

There is just one final thing holding us
back, then. It is that every man is his own
stickler. And while I am very much in fa-
vour of forming an army of well-informed
punctuation vigilantes, I can foresee prob-
lems getting everyone to pull in the same
direction. There will be those, for example,
who insist that the Oxford comma is an
abomination (the second comma in "ham,
eggs, and chips"), whereas others are unmoved by the Oxford comma but incensed
by the trend towards under-
hyphenation — which the Oxford comma
people have quite possibly never even noticed. Yes, as Evelyn Waugh wrote: "Everyone has always regarded any usage but
his own as either barbarous or pedantic."
Or, as Kingsley Amis put it less delicately
in his book *The King's English* (1997), the
world of grammar is divided into "berks
and wankers" — berks being those who are
outrageously slipshod about language, and
wankers those who are (in our view) ab-
horrently over-precise. Left to the berks,
the English language would "die of impu-

rity, like late Latin". Left to the wankers, it would die instead of purity, "like medieval Latin". Of course, the drawback is implicit. When you by nature subscribe to the view that everyone except yourself is a berk or a wanker, it is hard to bond with anybody in any rational common cause.

You think those thuggish chaps in movie heist gangs fall out a bit too quickly and mindlessly? Well, sticklers are worse. The Czech novelist Milan Kundera once fired a publisher who insisted on replacing a semicolon with a full stop; meanwhile, full-time editors working together on the same publication, using the same style book, will put hyphens in, take them out, and put them in again — all day, if necessary. The marginal direction to printers "STET" (meaning "let it stand" and cancelling an alteration) gets used rather a lot in these conditions. At *The Listener*, where I was literary editor from 1986 to 1990, I discovered that any efforts I made to streamline the prose on my pages would always be challenged by one particular sub-editor, who would proof-read my book reviews and archly insert literally dozens of little commas — each one of which I felt as a dart in my flesh. Of course, I never revealed the annoyance she caused. I would thank her, glance at the blizzard of marks on the galley proof, wait for her to leave the room, and then (standing up to get a better run at it) attack the proof, feverishly crossing out everything she had added, and writing "STET", "STET", "STET", "STET", "STET" all down the page, until my arm got tired and I was spent. And don't forget: this comma contention was not a matter of right or wrong. It was just a matter of taste.

Eats, Shoots & Leaves is not a book about grammar. I am not a grammarian. To me a subordinate clause will for ever be (since I heard the actor Martin Jarvis describe it thus) one of Santa's little helpers. A degree in English language is not a prerequisite for caring about where a bracket is preferred to a dash, or a comma needs to be replaced by a semicolon. If I did not believe that everyone is capable of understanding where an apostrophe goes, I would not be writing this book. Even as a book about punctuation, it will not give all the answers. There are already umpteen excellent punctuation guides on the market; there is even a rather delightful publication for children called *The Punctuation Repair Kit*, which takes the line "Hey! It's uncool to be stupid!" — which is a lie, of course, but you have to admire them for trying.

The trouble with all of these grammar books is that they are read principally by keen foreigners; meanwhile, native English-speakers who require their help are the last people who will make the effort to buy and read them. I am reminded of a scene in Woody Allen's *Small Time Crooks* when an oily Hugh Grant offers to help ignoramuses Allen and Tracey Ullman (newly wealthy) with any sort of cultural education. "Is there anything *you* want to know?" he asks Allen, who has been sullen throughout the interview. And Allen says reluctantly, "Well, I would like to learn how to spell Connecticut." What a great line that is. *I would like to learn how to spell Connecticut.* If you've similarly always wanted to know where to use an apostrophe, it means you never will, doesn't it? If only because it's so extremely easy to find out.

So if this book doesn't instruct about punctuation, what does it do? Well, you know those self-help books that give you permission to love yourself? This one gives you permission to love punctuation. It's about how we got the punctuation we have today; how such a tiny but adaptable system of marks allows us to notate most (but not all) types of verbal expression; and how (according to Beachcomber) a greengrocer in days of yore inspired Good Queen Bess to create the post of Apostropher Royal. But mainly it's about making sticklers feel good about their seventh-sense ability to see dead punctuation (whisper it in verge-of-tears tones: *"It doesn't know it's dead"*) and to defend their sense of humour. I have two cartoons I treasure. The first shows a row of ten Roman soldiers, one of them prone on the ground, with the cheerful caption (from a survivor of the cull), "Hey, this decimation isn't as bad as they say it is!" The second shows a bunch of vague, stupid-looking people standing outside a building, and behind them a big sign that says "Illiterates' Entrance". And do you want to know the awful truth? In the original drawing, it said, "Illiterate's Entrance", so I changed it. Painted correction fluid over the wrong apostrophe; inserted the right one. Yes, some of us were born to be punctuation vigilantes.

The Tractable Apostrophe

In the spring of 2001 the ITV1 show *Popstars* manufactured a pop phenomenon for our times: a singing group called Hear'Say. The announcement of the Hear'Say name was quite a national occasion, as I recall; people actually went out in very large numbers to buy their records; meanwhile, newspapers, who insist on precision in matters of address, at once learned to place Hear'Say's apostrophe correctly and attend to the proper spacing. To refer in print to this group as Hearsay (one word) would be wrong, you see. To call it Hear-Say (hyphenated) would show embarrassing ignorance of popular culture. And so it came to pass that Hear'Say's poor, oddly placed little apostrophe was replicated everywhere and no one gave a moment's thought to its sufferings. No one saw the pity of its position, hanging there in eternal meaninglessness, silently signalling to those with eyes to see, "I'm a legitimate punctuation mark, get me out of here." Checking the Hear'Say website a couple of years later, I discover that the only good news in this whole sorry saga was that, well, basically, once Kym had left to marry Jack in January 2002 — after rumours, counter-rumours and official denials — the group thankfully folded within eighteen months of its inception.

Now, there are no laws against imprisoning apostrophes and making them look daft. Cruelty to punctuation is quite unlegislated: you can get away with pulling the legs off semicolons; shrivelling question marks on the garden path under a powerful magnifying glass; you name it. But the naming of Hear'Say in 2001 was nevertheless a significant milestone on the road to punctuation anarchy. As we shall see, the tractable apostrophe has always done its proper jobs in our language with enthusiasm and elegance, but it has never been taken seriously enough; its talent for adaptability has been cruelly taken for granted; and now, in an age of supreme graphic frivolity, we pay the price. Too many jobs have been heaped on this tiny mark, and — far from complaining — the apostrophe has seemingly requested "More weight", just like that martyrish old codger in Arthur Miller's *The Crucible*, when religious bigots in black hats with buckles on are subjecting him to death by crushing. "More weight," the apostrophe has bravely said — if ever more faintly. "More weight," it manages to whisper still. But I ask you: how much more abuse must the apostrophe endure? Now that it's on its last legs (and idiotic showbiz promoters stick apostrophes in names for purely decorative purposes), isn't it time to recognise that the apostrophe needs our help?

The English language first picked up the apostrophe in the 16th century. The word in Greek means "turning away", and hence "omission" or "elision". In classical texts, it was used to mark dropped letters, as in *t'cius* for "tertius"; and when English printers adopted it, this was still its only function. Remember that comical pedant Holofernes in *Love's Labour's Lost* saying, "You find not the apostraphas, and so miss the accent"? Well, no, of course you don't, nobody remembers anything said by that frightful bore, and we certainly shan't detain ourselves bothering to work out what he was driving at. All we need to know is that, in Shakespeare's time, an apostrophe indicated omitted letters, which meant Hamlet could say with supreme apostrophic confidence: "Fie on't! O fie!"; " 'Tis a consummation devoutly to be wish'd"; and even, "I am too much i' the sun" — the latter, incidentally, a clear case of a writer employing a new-fangled punctuation mark entirely for the sake of it, and condemning countless generations of serious long-haired actors to adopt a knowing expression and say i' — as if this actually added anything to the meaning.

If only the apostrophe's life had stayed that simple. At some point in the 17th century, however, printers started to intrude an apostrophe before the "s" in singular possessive cases ("the girl's dress"), and from then on quite frankly the whole thing has spiralled into madness. In the 18th century, printers started to put it after plural possessives as well ("the girls' dresses"). Some historians of grammar claim, incidentally, that the original possessive use of the apostrophe signified a contraction of the historic "his"; and personally, I believed this attractive theory for many years, simply on the basis of knowing Ben Jonson's play *Sejanus, his Fall*, and reasoning that this was self-evidently halfway to "Sejanus's Fall". But blow me, if there aren't differences of opinion. There are other historians of grammar who say this Love-His-Labour-Is-Lost explanation is ignorant conjecture and should be forgotten as soon as heard.

Certainly the Henry-His-Wives (Henry's Wives) rationalisation falls down noticeably when applied to female possessives, because "Elizabeth Her Reign" would have ended up logically as "Elizabeth'r Reign", which would have had the regrettable result of making people sound a) a bit stupid, b) a bit drunk, or c) a bit from the West Country.

So what are the jobs an apostrophe currently has on its CV? Before we start tearing out our hair at sloppy, ignorant current usage, first let us acknowledge the sobering wisdom of the *Oxford Companion to English Literature*: "There never was a golden age in which the rules for the possessive apostrophe were clear-cut and known, understood and followed by most educated people." And then let us check that we know the rules of what modern grammarians call "possessive determiners" and "possessive pronouns" — *none of which requires an apostrophe.*

Possessive determiners

my	our
your	your
his	their
her	their
its	their

Possessive pronouns

mine	ours
yours	yours
his	theirs
hers	theirs
its	theirs

And now, let us just count the various important tasks the apostrophe is obliged to execute every day.

1 It indicates a possessive in a singular noun:
The boy's hat
The First Lord of the Admiralty's rather smart front door

This seems simple. But not so fast, Batman. When the possessor is plural, but does not end in an "s", the apostrophe similarly precedes the "s":

The children's playground
The women's movement

But when the possessor is a regular plural, the apostrophe follows the "s":

The boys' hats (more than one boy)
The babies' bibs

I apologise if you know all this, but the point is many, many people do not. Why else would they open a large play area for children, hang up a sign saying "Giant Kid's Playground", and then wonder why everyone stays away from it? (Answer: everyone is scared of the Giant Kid.)

2 *It indicates time or quantity:*
In one week's time
Four yards' worth
Two weeks' notice (Warner Brothers, take note)

3 *It indicates the omission of figures in dates:*
The summer of '68

4 *It indicates the omission of letters:*
We can't go to Jo'burg (We cannot go to Johannesburg — perhaps because we can't spell the middle bit)
She'd've had the cat-o'-nine-tails, I s'pose, if we hadn't stopped 'im (She would have had a right old lashing, I reckon, if we had not intervened)

However, it is generally accepted that familiar contractions such as bus (omnibus), flu (influenza), phone (telephone), photo (photograph) and cello (violoncello) no longer require apologetic apostrophes. In fact to write "Any of that wine left in the 'fridge, dear?" looks today self-conscious, not to say poncey. Other contractions have made the full leap into new words, anyway. There is simply nowhere to hang an apostrophe on "nuke" (explode a nuclear device), "telly" (television) or "pram" (perambulator) – although, believe me, people have tried.

Most famously of all, the apostrophe of omission creates the word "it's":

It's your turn (it is your turn)
It's got very cold (it has got very cold)
It's a braw bricht moonlicht nicht the
    nicht (no idea)

To those who care about punctuation, a sentence such as "Thank God its Friday" (without the apostrophe) rouses feelings not only of despair but of violence. The confusion of the possessive "its" (no apostrophe) with the contractive "it's" (with apostrophe) is an unequivocal signal of illiteracy and sets off a simple Pavlovian "kill" response in the average stickler. The rule is: the word "it's" (with apostrophe) stands for "it is" or "it has". If the word does not stand for "it is" or "it has" then what you require is "its". *This is extremely easy to grasp.* Getting your itses mixed up is the greatest solecism in the world of punctuation. No matter that you have a PhD and have read all of Henry James twice. If you still persist in writing, "Good food at it's best", you deserve to be struck by lightning, hacked up on the spot and buried in an unmarked grave.

5 *It indicates strange, non-standard English:* A forest of apostrophes in dialogue (often accompanied by unusual capitalisation) conventionally signals the presence in a text of a peasant, a cockney or an earnest northerner from whom the heart-chilling word "nobbut" may soon be heard. Here is what the manly gamekeeper Mellors says to his employer's wife in chapter eight of D. H. Lawrence's *Lady Chatterley's Lover*:

" 'Appen yer'd better 'ave this key, an' Ah min fend for t' bods some other road . . . 'Appen Ah can find anuther pleece as'll du for rearin' th' pheasants. If yer want ter be 'ere, yo'll non want me messin' abaht a' th' time."

"Why don't you speak ordinary English?" Lady Chatterley inquires, saucily.

6 It features in Irish names such as O'Neill and O'Casey:

Again the theory that this is a simple contraction — this time of "of" (as in John o' Gaunt) — is pure woolly misconception. Not a lot of people know this, but the "O" in Irish names is an anglicisation of "ua", meaning grandson.

7 It indicates the plurals of letters:

How many f's are there in Fulham? (Larky answer, beloved of football fans: there's only one f in Fulham)

In the winter months, his R's blew off (old Peter Cook and Dudley Moore joke, explaining the mysterious zoo sign "T OPICAL FISH, THIS WAY")

8 It also indicates plurals of words:

What are the do's and don't's?

Are there too many but's and and's at the beginnings of sentences these days?

,

I hope that by now you are already feeling sorry for the apostrophe. Such a list of legitimate apostrophe jobs certainly brings home to us the imbalance of responsibility that exists in the world of punctuation. I mean, full stops are quite important, aren't they? Yet by contrast to the versatile apostrophe, they are stolid little chaps, to say the least. In fact one might dare to say that while the full stop is the lumpen male of the punctuation world (do one job at a time; do it well; forget about it instantly), the apostrophe is the frantically multi-tasking female, dotting hither and yon, and succumbing to burnout from all the thankless effort. Only one significant task has been lifted from the apostrophe's workload in recent years: it no longer has to appear in the plurals of abbreviations ("MPs") or plural dates ("1980s"). Until quite recently, it was customary to write "MP's" and "1980's" — and in fact this convention still applies in America. British readers of *The New Yorker* who assume that this august publication is in constant ignorant error when it allows "1980's" evidently have no experience of how that famously punctilious periodical operates editorially.

But it is in the nature of punctuation lovers to care about such things, and I applaud all those who seek to protect the apostrophe from misuse. For many years

Keith Waterhouse operated an Association for the Abolition of the Aberrant Apostrophe in the *Daily Mirror* and then the *Daily Mail*, cheered on by literally millions of readers. He has printed hundreds of examples of apostrophe horrors, my all-time favourite being the rather subtle, "Prudential — were here to help you", which looks just a bit unsettling until you realise that what it's supposed to say is, "Prudential — *we're* here to help you". And Keith Waterhouse has many successors in the print. Kevin Myers, columnist of *The Irish Times*, recently published a fictional story about a man who joins the League of Signwriter's and Grocer's and Butcher's Assistant's, only to discover that his girlfriend is a stickler for grammatical precision.

Meanwhile, William Hartston, who writes the "Beachcomber" column in *The Express*, has come up with the truly inspired story of the Apostropher Royal, an ancient and honourable post inaugurated in the reign of Queen Elizabeth I. His story goes that a humble greengrocer (in days of yore) was delivering potatoes to Good Queen Bess and happened to notice a misplaced apostrophe in a royal decree. When he pointed it out, the Queen immediately created the office of Apostropher Royal, to control the quality and distribution of apostrophes and deliver them in wheelbarrows to all the greengrocers of England on the second Thursday of every month (Apostrophe Thursday). The present Apostropher Royal, Sir D'Anville O'M'Darlin', concerns himself these days with such urgent issues as the tendency of "trendy publishers" to replace quotation marks with colons and dashes, the effect of which is that pairs of unwanted inverted commas can be illegally shipped abroad, split down the middle to form low-grade apostrophes and sold back to an unwary British public.

Do people other than professional writers care, though? Well, yes, and I have proof in heaps. As I was preparing for this book, I wrote an article for *The Daily Telegraph*, hoping to elicit a few punctuation horror stories, and it was like detonating a dam. Hundreds of emails and letters arrived, all of them testifying to the astonishing power of recall we sticklers have when things have annoyed us ("It was in 1987, I'll never forget, and it said "CREAM TEA'S"); and also to the justifiable despair of the well educated in a dismally illiterate world. Reading the letters, I was alternately thrilled that so many people had bothered to write and sunk low by such overwhelming evidence of Britain's stupidity and indifference. The vast majority of letters concerned misplaced apostrophes, of course, in *potato's* and *lemon's*. But it was interesting, once I started to analyse and sort the examples, to discover that the greengrocer's apostrophe formed just one depressing category of the overall, total, mind-bogglingly depressing misuse of the apostrophe. Virtually every proper application of this humble mark utterly stumps the people who write to us officially, who paint signs, or who sell us fruit and veg. The following is just a tiny selection of the examples I received:

Singular possessive instead of simple plural (the "greengrocer's apostrophe"):
Trouser's reduced
Coastguard Cottage's
Next week: nouns and apostrophe's!
   (BBC website advertising a grammar course for children)

Singular possessive instead of plural possessive:
Pupil's entrance (on a very selective school, presumably)

Adult Learner's Week (lucky him)

Frog's Piss (French wine putting unfair strain on single frog)

Member's May Ball (but with whom will the member dance?)

Nude Reader's Wives (intending "Readers' Nude Wives", of course, but conjuring up an interesting picture of polygamous nude reader attended by middle-aged women in housecoats and fluffy slippers)

Plural possessive instead of singular possessive:

Lands' End (mail-order company which roundly denies anything wrong with name)

Bobs' Motors

No possessive where possessive is required:
Citizens Advice Bureau
Mens Toilets
Britains Biggest Junction (Clapham)

Dangling expectations caused by incorrect pluralisation:
Pansy's ready (is she?)
Cyclist's only (his only what?)
Please replace the trolley's (replace the trolley's what?)

and best of all:

> Nigger's out (a sign seen in New York, under which was written, wickedly: "But he'll be back shortly")

Unintentional sense from unmarked possessive:
Dicks in tray (try not to think about it)
New members welcome drink (doubtless true)

Someone knows an apostrophe is required . . . but where, oh where?
It need'nt be a pane (on a van advertising discount glass)
Ladie's hairdresser
Mens coat's
Childrens' education . . . (in a letter from the head of education at the National Union of Teachers)
The Peoples Princess' (on memorial mug)
Freds' restaurant

Apostrophes put in place names/proper names:
Dear Mr Steven's
XMA'S TREES
Glady's (badge on salesgirl)
Did'sbury

It's or Its' instead of Its:

Hundreds of examples, many from respectable National Trust properties and big corporations, but notably:

Hot Dogs a Meal in Its' Self (sign in Great Yarmouth)

Recruitment at it's best (slogan of employment agency)

". . . to welcome you to the British Library, it's services and catalogues" (reader induction pamphlet at British Library)

Plain illiteracy:

". . . giving the full name and title of the person who's details are given in Section 02" (on UK passport application form)

Make our customer's live's easier (Abbey National advertisement)

Gateaux's (evidently never spelled any other way)

Your 21 today! (on birthday card)

Commas instead of apostrophes:

Antique,s (on A120 near Colchester)

apples,s

orange,s

grape,s (all thankfully on the same stall)

Signs that have given up trying:
Reader offer
Author photograph
Customer toilet

This is a mere sample of the total I received. I heard from people whose work colleagues used commas instead of apostrophes; from someone rather thoughtfully recommending a restaurant called l'Apostrophe in Reims (address on request); and from a Somerset man who had cringed regularly at a sign on a market garden until he discovered that its proprietor's name was — you couldn't make it up — R. Carrott. This explained why the sign said "Carrott's" at the top, you see, but then listed other vegetables and fruits spelled and punctuated perfectly correctly.

,

Up to now, we have looked at the right and wrong uses of the apostrophe, and I have felt on pretty safe ground. All this is about to change, however, because there are areas of apostrophe use that are not so simple, and we must now follow the apostrophe as it flits innocently into murky tunnels of style, usage and (oh no!) acceptable exception. Take the possessive of proper names ending in "s" – such as my own. Is this properly "Lynne Truss' book" or "Lynne Truss's book"? One correspondent (whose name I have changed) wrote with a tone of impatience: "From an early age I knew that if I wanted to write Philippa Jones' book I did NOT WRITE Philippa Jones's book with a second 's'. I see this error often even on a school minibus: St James's School. Perhaps the rules have changed or the teachers just do not know nowadays."

Sadly, this correspondent has been caught in the embarrassing position of barking up two wrong trees at the same time; but only because tastes have changed in the matter. Current guides to punctuation (including that ultimate authority, *Fowler's Modern English Usage*) state that with modern names ending in "s" (including biblical names, and any foreign name with an unpronounced final "s"), the "s" *is* required after the apostrophe:

Keats's poems
Philippa Jones's book
St James's Square
Alexander Dumas's *The Three Musketeers*

With names from the ancient world, it is not:

Archimedes' screw
Achilles' heel

If the name ends in an "iz" sound, an exception is made:

Bridges' score
Moses' tablets

And an exception is always made for Jesus:

Jesus' disciples

However, these are matters of style and preference that are definitely not set in stone, and it's a good idea not to get fixated about them. Bill Walsh's charmingly titled book *Lapsing into a Comma* (Walsh is a copy desk chief at *The Washington Post*) explains that while many American newspapers prefer "Connors' forehand", his own preference is for "Connors's forehand" — "and I'm happy to be working for a newspaper that feels the same way I do". Consulting a dozen or so recently published punctuation guides, I can report that they contain minor disagreements on virtually all aspects of the above and that their only genuine consistency is in using Keats's poems as the prime example. Strange, but true. They just can't leave Keats alone. "It is *Keats' poems* (NOT *Keats's*)," they thunder. Or alternatively: "It is *Keats's poems* (NOT *Keats'*)." Well, poor old Keats, you can't help thinking. No wonder he developed that cough.

Having said that there are no absolute rights and wrongs in this matter, however, when many people wrote to ask why St Thomas' Hospital in London has no "s" after the apostrophe, I did feel that the answer must echo Dr Johnson's when asked to explain his erroneous definition of a pastern: "Ignorance, madam, pure ignorance." Of course it should be St Thomas's Hospital. *Of course it should.* The trouble is that institutions, towns, colleges, families, companies and brands have authority over their own spelling and punctuation (which is often historic), and there is absolutely nothing we can do except raise an eyebrow and make a mental note. Virtually the first things a British newspaper sub-editor learns are that Lloyds TSB (the bank) has no apostrophe, unlike Lloyd's of London (insurance); Earls Court, Gerrards Cross and St Andrews have no apostrophe (although Earl's Court tube station seems to have acquired one); HarperCollins has no space; Bowes Lyon has no hyphen; and you have to give initial capitals to the words Biro and Hoover otherwise you automatically get tedious letters from solicitors, reminding you that these are brand names. The satirical magazine *Private Eye* once printed one of the letters from Biro's representatives, incidentally, under the memorable heading, "What a pathetic way to make a living".

St Thomas' Hospital is thus the self-styled name of the hospital and that's that. The stadium of Newcastle United FC is, similarly, St James' Park. In the end, neither example is worth getting worked up about — in fact, on the contrary, once you have taken a few deep breaths, you may find it within you not only to tolerate these exceptions but positively to treasure them and even love them. Personally, I now lose all power of speech if I see University College London ignorantly awarded a comma where none belongs, or E. M. Forster's title *Howards End* made to look ordinary by some itchy-fingered proofreader. Meanwhile, *The Times Guide to English Style and Usage* (1999) sensibly advises its readers not to pin their mental well-being on such matters, putting it beautifully: "Beware of organisations that have apostrophe variations as their house style, eg, St Thomas' Hospital, where we must respect their whim."

It is time to confess that I have for many years struggled with one of the lesser rules of the apostrophe. I refer to the "double possessive", which is evidently a perfectly respectable grammatical construction, but simply jars with me, and perhaps always will. We see it all the time in newspapers:

> "Elton John, a friend of the footballer's, said last night . . ."
> "Elton John, a friend of the couple's, said last night . . ."
> "Elton John, a friend of the Beckhams', said last night . . ."

Well, pass me the oxygen, Elton, and for heaven's sake, stop banging on about your glitzy mates for a minute while I think. *A friend of the footballer's?* Why isn't it, "a friend of the footballer"? Doesn't the construction "of the" do away with the need for another possessive? I mean to say, why do those sweet little Beckhams need to possess Elton John twice? Or is that a silly question?

But fight the mounting panic and turn to Robert Burchfield's third edition of *Fowler's Modern English Usage* (1998), and what do I find? The double possessive is calmly explained, and I start to peel away the problem. Do I have any objection to the construction "a friend of mine" or "a friend of yours"? Well, no. I would never say "a friend of me" or "a friend of you". And yes, you *would* say "a cousin of my mother's", "a child of hers". Well, "a friend of the footballer's" is the same thing! The only time you drop the double possessive is when, instead of being involved with an animate being, you are "a lover of the British Museum", because obviously the British Museum does not — and never can — love you back.

We may all be getting a little sick and tired of the apostrophe by now, so I'll just get a couple more things off my chest.

1 Someone wrote to say that my use of "one's" was wrong ("a common error"), and that it should be *ones*. This is such rubbish that I refuse to argue about it. Go and tell Virginia Woolf it should be *A Room of Ones Own* and see how far you get.

2 To reiterate, if you can replace the word with "it is" or "it has", then the word is *it's:*

It's a long way to Tipperary.

If you can replace the word with "who is" or "who has", then the word is *who's:*

Who's that knocking at my door?

If you can replace the word with "they are", then the word is *they're:*

They're not going to get away with this.

And if you can replace the word with "there is", the word is *there's:*

There's a surprising amount about the apostrophe in this book.

If you can replace the word with "you are", then the word is *you're:*

You're never going to forget the difference between "its" and "it's".

We may curse our bad luck that *it's* sounds

like *its; who's* sounds like *whose; they're* sounds like *their* (and *there*); *there's* sounds like *theirs;* and *you're* sounds like *your.* But if we are grown-ups who have been through full-time education, we have no excuse for muddling them up.

This chapter is nearing its end.
Whose book is this, again?
Some of *their* suggestions were outrageous!
This is no concern of *theirs!*
Your friend Elton John has been talking about you again.

,

In Beachcomber's hilarious columns about the Apostropher Royal in *The Express,* a certain perversely comforting law is often reiterated: the Law of Conservation of Apostrophes. A heresy since the 13th century, this law states that a balance exists in nature: "For every apostrophe omitted from an *it's,* there is an extra one put into an *its.*" Thus the number of apostrophes in circulation remains constant, even if this means we have double the reason to go and bang our heads against a wall.

The only illiteracy with apostrophes that

stirs any sympathy in me is the greengrocer's variety. First, because greengrocers are self-evidently horny-thumbed people who do not live by words. And second, because I agree with them that something rather troubling and unsatisfactory happens to words ending in vowels when you just plonk an "s" on the end. Take the word "bananas": at first glance, you might suppose that the last syllable is pronounced "ass". How can the word "banana" keep its pronunciation when pluralised? Well, you could stick an apostrophe before the "s"! Obviously there is no excuse for not knowing "potatoes" is the plural of "potato", but if you were just to put an "s" after it, the impulse to separate it from the "o" with some mark or other would be pretty compelling, because "potatos" would be pronounced, surely, "pot-at-oss".

Moreover, what many people don't know, as they fulminate against ignorant greengrocers, is that until the 19th century this was one of the legitimate uses of the apostrophe: to separate a plural "s" from a foreign word ending in a vowel, and thus prevent confusion about pronunciation. Thus, you would see in an 18th-century text *folio's* or *quarto's* — and it looks rather elegant. I just wish a different mark had been employed (or even invented) for the purpose, to take the strain off our long-suffering little friend; and I hear, in fact, that there are moves afoot among certain punctuation visionaries to revive the practice using the tilde (the Spanish accent we all have on our keyboards which looks like this: ˜). Thus: *quarto˜s* and *folio˜s,* not to mention *logo˜s, pasta˜s, ouzo˜s* and *banana˜s.* For the time being, however, the guardians of usage frown very deeply on anyone writing "quarto's". As Professor Loreto Todd tartly remarks in her excellent *Cassell's Guide to Punctuation* (1995), "This usage was correct once, just as it was once considered correct to drink tea from a saucer."

It would be nice if one day the number of apostrophes properly placed in *it's* equalled exactly the number of apostrophes properly omitted from *its,* instead of the other way round. In the meantime, what can be done by those of us sickened by the state of apostrophe abuse? First, we must refute the label "dinosaurs" (I really hate that). And second, we must take up arms. Here are the weapons required in the apostrophe war (stop when you start to feel uncomfortable):

correction fluid

big pens

stickers cut in a variety of sizes, both plain (for sticking over unwanted apostrophes) and coloured (for inserting where apostrophes are needed)

tin of paint with big brush

guerrilla-style clothing

strong medication for personality disorder

loudhailer

gun

Evidently there used to be a shopkeeper in Bristol who deliberately stuck ungrammatical signs in his window as a ruse to draw people into the shop; they would come in to complain, and he would then talk them into buying something. Well, he would be ill-advised to repeat this ploy once my punctuation vigilantes are on the loose. We lovers of the apostrophe will not stand by and let it be abolished — not because we are dinosaurs who drink tea out of saucers (interesting image) but because we appreciate the way the apostrophe has for centuries graced our words and illuminated our meaning. It is no fault of the apostrophe that some of our words need so much help identifying themselves. Indeed, it is to the credit of the apostrophe that it can manage the task. Those spineless types who talk about abolishing the apostrophe are missing the point, and the pun is very much intended. The next day after the abolition of the apostrophe, imagine the scene. Triumphant abolitionist sits down to write, "Goodbye to the Apostrophe: we're not missing you a bit!" and finds that he can't. Abolish the apostrophe and it will be necessary, before the hour is up, to reinvent it.

That'll Do, Comma

When the humorist James Thurber was writing for *New Yorker* editor Harold Ross in the 1930s and 1940s, the two men often had very strong words about commas. It is pleasant to picture the scene: two hard-drinking alpha males in serious trilbies smacking a big desk and barking at each other over the niceties of punctuation. According to Thurber's account of the matter (in *The Years with Ross* [1959]), Ross's "clarification complex" tended to run somewhat to the extreme: he seemed to believe there was no limit to the amount of clarification you could achieve if you just kept adding commas. Thurber, by self-appointed virtuous contrast, saw commas as so many upturned office chairs unhelpfully hurled down the wide-open corridor of readability. And so they endlessly disagreed. If Ross were to write "red, white, and blue" with the maximum number of commas, Thurber would defiantly state a preference for "red white and blue" with none at all, on the provocative grounds that "all those commas make the flag seem rained on. They give it a furled look."

If you want to know about editorial "commaphilia" as a source of chronic antagonism, read *The Years with Ross*. Thurber once went so far as to send Ross a few typed lines of one of Wordsworth's *Lucy* poems, repunctuated in *New Yorker* style:

She lived, alone, and few could know
When Lucy ceased to be,
But, she is in her grave, and, oh,
The difference, to me.

But Ross, it seems, was unmoved by sarcasm, and in the end Thurber simply had to resign himself to Ross's way of thinking. After all, he was the boss; he signed the cheques; and of course he was a brilliant editor, who endearingly admitted once in a letter to H. L. Mencken, "We have carried editing to a very high degree of fussiness here, probably to a point approaching the ultimate. I don't know how to get it under control." And so the comma proliferated. Thurber was once asked by a correspondent: "Why did you have a comma in the sentence, 'After dinner, the men went into the living-room'?" And his answer was probably one of the loveliest things ever said about punctuation. "This particular comma," Thurber explained, "was Ross's way of giving the men time to push back their chairs and stand up."

Why the problem? Why the scope for such differences of opinion? Aren't there rules for the comma, just as there are rules for the apostrophe? Well, yes; but you will be entertained to discover that there is a significant complication in the case of the comma. More than any other mark, the comma draws our attention to the mixed origins of modern punctuation, and its consequent mingling of two quite distinct functions:

1 To illuminate the grammar of a sentence

2 To point up — rather in the manner of musical notation — such literary qualities as rhythm, direction, pitch, tone and flow

This is why grown men have knockdown fights over the comma in editorial offices: because these two roles of punctuation sometimes collide head-on — indeed, where the comma is concerned, they do it all the time. In 1582, Richard Mulcaster's

The First Part of the Elementarie (an early English grammar) described the comma as "a small crooked point, which in writing followeth some small branch of the sentence, & in reading warneth vs to rest there, & to help our breth a little". Many subsequent grammars of the 17th, 18th and 19th centuries make the same distinction. When Ross and Thurber were threatening each other with ashtrays over the correct way to render the star-spangled banner, they were reflecting a deep dichotomy in punctuation that had been around and niggling people for over four hundred years. On the page, punctuation performs its grammatical function, but in the mind of the reader it does more than that. It tells the reader how to hum the tune.

,

If only we hadn't started reading quietly to ourselves. Things were so simple at the start, before grammar came along and ruined things. The earliest known punctuation — credited to Aristophanes of Byzantium (librarian at Alexandria) around 200 BC — was a three-part system of dramatic notation (involving single points at different heights on the line) advising actors when to breathe in preparation for a long bit, or a not-so-long bit, or a relatively short bit. And that's all there was to it. A *comma,* at that time, was the name of the relatively short bit (the word means in Greek "a piece cut off"); and in fact when the word "comma" was adopted into English in the 16th century, it still referred to a discrete, separable group of words rather than the friendly little tadpoley number-nine dot-with-a-tail that today we know and love. For a millennium and a half, punctuation's purpose was to guide actors, chanters and readers-aloud through stretches of manuscript, indicating the pauses, accentuating matters of sense and sound, and leaving syntax mostly to look after itself. St Jerome, who translated the Bible in the 4th century, introduced a system of punctuation of religious texts *per cola et commata* ("by phrases"), to aid accurate pausing when reading aloud. Cassiodorus, writing in the 6th century in southern Italy for the guidance of trainee scribes, included punctuation in his *Institutiones Divinarum et Saecularium Litterarum,* recommending "clear pausing in well-regulated delivery". I do hope Harold Pinter knows about all this, by the way;

who would have thought the pause had such a long and significant history?

Most of the marks used by those earnest scribes look bizarre to us now, of course: the *positura,* a mark like a number 7, which indicated the end of a piece of text; the sinister mark like the little gallows in a game of hangman that indicated the start of a paragraph (paragraphs weren't indented until much later); and, significantly here, the *virgula suspensiva,* which looked like our present-day *solidus* or forward slash (/), and was used to mark the briefest pause or hesitation. Perhaps the key thing one needs to realise about the early history of punctuation is that, in a literary culture based entirely on the slavish copying of venerated texts, it would be highly presumptuous of a mere scribe to insert helpful marks where he thought they ought to go. Punctuation developed slowly and cautiously not because it wasn't considered important, but, on the contrary, because it was such intensely powerful ju-ju. Pause in the wrong place and the sense of a religious text can alter in significant ways. For example, as Cecil Hartley pointed out in his 1818 *Principles of Punctuation: or, The Art of Pointing,* consider the difference between the following:

"Verily, I say unto thee, This day thou shalt be with me in Paradise."

and:

"Verily I say unto thee this day, Thou shalt be with me in Paradise."

Now, huge doctrinal differences hang on the placing of this comma. The first version, which is how Protestants interpret the passage (Luke, xxiii, 43), lightly skips over the whole unpleasant business of Purgatory and takes the crucified thief straight to heaven with Our Lord. The second promises Paradise at some later date (to be confirmed, as it were) and leaves Purgatory nicely in the picture for the Catholics, who believe in it. Similarly, it is argued that the Authorised Version of the Bible (and by extension Handel's *Messiah*) misleads on the true interpretation of Isaiah xl, 3. Again, consider the difference:

"The voice of him that crieth in the wilderness: Prepare ye the way of the Lord."

and:

"The voice of him that crieth: In the

wilderness prepare ye the way of the Lord."

Also:

"Comfort ye my people"
(please go out and comfort my people)

and

"Comfort ye, my people"
(just cheer up, you lot; it might never happen)

Of course, if Hebrew or any of the other ancient languages had included punctuation (in the case of Hebrew, a few vowels might have been nice as well), two thousand years of scriptural exegesis need never have occurred, and a lot of clever, dandruffy people could definitely have spent more time in the fresh air. But there was no punctuation in those ancient texts and that's all there is to it. For a considerable period in Latin transcriptions there were no gaps between words either, if you can credit such madness. Texts from that benighted classical period — just capital letters in big square blocks — look to modern eyes like those word-search puzzles that you stare at for twenty minutes or so, and then (with a delighted cry) suddenly spot the word "PAPERNAPKIN" spelled diagonally and backwards. However, the *scriptio continua* system (as it was called) had its defenders at the time. One fifth-century recluse called Cassian argued that if a text was slow to offer up its meaning, this encouraged not only healthy meditation but the glorification of God — the heart lifting in praise, obviously, at the moment when the word "PAPER-NAPKIN" suddenly floated to the surface, like a synaptic miracle.

Isn't this history interesting? Well, I think so — even though, for a considerable time, admittedly, not much happened. That imaginative chap Charlemagne (forward-looking Holy Roman Emperor) stirred things up in the 9th century when Alcuin of York came up with a system of *positurae* at the ends of sentences (including one of the earliest question marks), but to be honest western systems of punctuation were damned unsatisfactory for the next five hundred years until one man — one fabulous Venetian printer — finally wrestled with the issue and pinned it to the mat. That man was Aldus Manutius the Elder (1450–1515) and I will happily admit I hadn't heard of him until about a year ago, but am now absolutely kicking myself that I never volunteered to have his babies.

The heroic status of Aldus Manutius the Elder among historians of the printed word cannot be overstated. Who invented the italic typeface? Aldus Manutius! Who printed the first semicolon? Aldus Manutius! The rise of printing in the 14th and 15th centuries meant that a standard system of punctuation was urgently required, and Aldus Manutius was the man to do it. In *Pause and Effect* (1992), Malcolm Parkes's magisterial account of the history of punctuation in the West, facsimile examples of Aldus's ground-breaking work include a page from Pietro Bembo's *De Aetna* (1494) which features not only a very elegant roman typeface but the actual first semicolon (and believe me, this is exciting). Of course we did not get our modern system overnight, but Aldus Manutius and his grandson (conveniently of the same name) are generally credited with developing several of our modern conventional signs. They lowered the *virgule* and curved it, for a start, so that it began to look like the modern comma. They put colons and full stops at the ends of sentences. Like this. And also — less comfortably to the modern eye — like this:

Most significantly of all, however, they ignored the old marks that had aided the reader-aloud. Books were now for reading and understanding, not intoning. Moving your lips was becoming a no-no. Within the seventy years it took for Aldus Manutius the Elder to be replaced by Aldus Manutius the Younger, things changed so drastically that in 1566 Aldus Manutius the Younger was able to state that the main object of punctuation was the clarification of syntax. Forget all that stuff about the spiritual value to the reader of working out the meaning for himself; forget as well the humility of those copyists of old. I'm sure people did question whether Italian printers were quite the right people to legislate on the meaning of everything; but on the other hand, *resistance was obviously useless against a family that could invent italics.*

So what happened to the comma in this process? Well, between the 16th century and the present day, it became a kind of scary grammatical sheepdog. As we shall shortly see, the comma has so many jobs as a "separator" (punctuation marks are traditionally either "separators" or "terminators") that it tears about on the hillside of language, endlessly organising words into sensible groups and making them stay put: sorting and dividing; circling and herding; and of course darting off with a peremptory "woof" to round up any wayward subordinate clause that makes a futile bolt for semantic freedom. Commas, if you don't whistle at them to calm down, are unstoppably enthusiastic at this job. Luckily the trend in the 20th century (starting with H. W. Fowler's *The King's English* in 1906) has been towards ever-simpler punctuation, with fewer and fewer commas; but take any passage from a non-contemporary writer and you can't help seeing the constituent words as so many defeated sheep that have been successfully corralled with the gate slammed shut by good old Comma the Sheepdog.

Jones flung himself at his benefactor's feet, and taking eagerly hold of his hand, assured him, his goodness to him, both now, and at all other times, had so infinitely exceeded not only his merit, but his hopes, that no words could express his sense of it.
Henry Fielding, *Tom Jones*, 1749

It needed a quick eye to detect, from among the huddled mass of sleepers, the form of any given individual. As they lay closely packed together, covered, for warmth's sake, with their patched and ragged clothes, little could be distinguished but the sharp outlines of pale faces, over which sombre light shed the same dull, heavy colour, with here and there a gaunt arm thrust forth, its thinness hidden by no covering, but fully exposed to view, in all its shrunken ugliness.

Charles Dickens,
Nicholas Nickleby, 1839

No wonder feelings run high about the comma. When it comes to improving the clarity of a sentence, you can nearly always argue that one should go in; you can nearly always argue that one should come out. Stylists have meanwhile always dickered with the rules: Oscar Wilde famously spent all day on a completed poem, dangling a questionable comma over it; Gertrude Stein called the comma "servile" and refused to have anything to do with it; Peter Carey cleverly won the Booker Prize in 2001 for a book that contained no commas at all (*True History of the Kelly Gang*); and I have seen an essay on the internet seriously accusing John Updike, that wicked man, of bending the rules of the comma to his own ends "with fragments, comma splices, coordinate clauses without commas, ellipted coordinate clauses with commas, *and more*" — charges to which, of course, those of us with no idea what an ellipted-coordinate-clause-with-a-comma might look like can only comment, "Tsk".

Meanwhile, lawyers eschew the comma as far as possible, regarding it as a trouble-maker; and readers grow so accustomed to the dwindling incidence of commas in public places that when signs go up saying "No dogs please", only one person in a thousand bothers to point out that actually, as a statement, "no dogs please" is an indefensible generalisation, since many dogs *do* please, as a matter of fact; they rather make a point of it.

,

"The use of commas cannot be learned by rule." Such was the opinion of the great Sir Ernest Gowers; and I have to say I find that a comfort, coming from the grand old boy himself. However, rules certainly exist for the comma and we may as well examine some of them.

The fun of commas is of course the semantic havoc they can create when either wrongly inserted ("What is this thing called, love?") or carelessly omitted ("He shot himself as a child").* A friend of mine who runs a Shakespeare reading group in New England tells a delightful story of a chap playing Duncan in *Macbeth* who listened with appropriate pity and concern while the wounded soldier in Act I gave his account of the battle, and then cheerfully called out, "Go get him, surgeons!" (It's supposed to be "Go, get him surgeons.")

But we'll come to such lovely enjoyable things by and by. In the meantime, however, this is serious. Sharpen a pencil, line up your favourite stimulants, furrow the brow, and attempt to concentrate on the following.

1. Commas for lists

This is probably the first thing you ever learn about commas, that they divide items in lists, but are not required before the *and* on the end:

---

*He shot, himself, as a child.

The four refreshing fruit flavours of Opal Fruits are orange, lemon, strawberry and lime.

I had a marvellous time eating in tavernas, swimming in the turquoise water, getting sloshed on retsina and not sending postcards.

The colours of the Union Jack are red, white and blue.

The rule here is that the comma is correct if it can be replaced by the word *and* or *or*. For example: "I had a marvellous time eating in tavernas *and* swimming in the turquoise water *and* getting sloshed on retsina and not sending postcards." This would be the grammatical consequence of omitting the comma: a sentence that is clumsy (and sounds a lot more sloshed), but still counts as grammatical. What a loss to the language it was, incidentally, when they changed the name of Opal Fruits to Starburst.

However, if you feel you are safe paddling in these sparklingly clear shallows of comma usage, think again. See that comma-shaped shark fin ominously slicing through the waves in this direction? Hear that staccato cello? Well, start waving and yelling, because it is the so-called Oxford comma (also known as the serial comma) and it is a lot more dangerous than its exclusive, ivory-tower moniker might suggest. There are people who embrace the Oxford comma and people who don't, and I'll just say this: *never* get between these people when drink has been taken. Oh, the Oxford comma. Here, in case you don't know what it is yet, is the perennial example, as espoused by Harold Ross: "The flag is red, white, and blue."

So what do you think of it? (It's the comma after "white".) Are you for it or against it? Do you hover in between? In Britain, where standard usage is to leave it out, there are those who put it in — including, interestingly, *Fowler's Modern English Usage*. In America, conversely, where standard usage is to leave it in, there are those who make a point of removing it (especially journalists). British grammarians will concede that sometimes the extra comma prevents confusion, as when there are other *and*s in the vicinity:

I went to the chemist, Marks & Spencer, and NatWest.
I went to NatWest, the chemist, and Marks & Spencer.

But this isn't much of a concession, when you think about it. My own feeling is that one shouldn't be too rigid about the Oxford comma. Sometimes the sentence is improved by including it; sometimes it isn't. For example, in the introduction to this book (page 33) I allude to punctuation marks as the traffic signals of language: "they tell us to slow down, notice this, take a detour, and stop". And, well, I argued for that Oxford comma. It seemed to me that without the comma after "detour", this was a list of three instructions (the last a double one), not four. And here was a case where the stylistic reasons for its inclusion clearly outweighed the grammatical ones for taking it out. This was a decelerating sentence. The commas were incrementally applying the brakes. To omit the comma after "detour" would have the sentence suddenly coasting at speed again instead of slowing to the final halt.

Anyway, there are some more points about commas in lists before we move on. In a list of adjectives, again the rule is that you use a comma where an *and* would be appropriate — where the modifying words are all modifying the same thing to the same degree:

It was a dark, stormy night. (The night was dark and stormy)

He was a tall, bearded man. (The man was tall and bearded)

But you do NOT use a comma for:

It was an endangered white rhino.

Australian red wines are better than Australian white ones.

The grand old Duke of York had ten thousand men.

This is because, in each of these cases, the adjectives do their jobs in joyful combination; they are not intended as a list. The rhino isn't endangered *and* white. The wines aren't Australian *and* red. The Duke of York wasn't grand *and* old. The wedding wasn't big *and* fat *and* Greek.

2. Commas for joining

Commas are used when two complete sentences are joined together, using such conjunctions as *and, or, but, while* and *yet*:

The boys wanted to stay up until midnight, but they grew tired and fell asleep.

> I thought I had the biggest bag of Opal
> Fruits, yet Cathy proved me wrong.

If this seems a bit obvious to you, I apologise. But trouble arises with this joining-comma rule from two directions: when stylists deliberately omit the conjunction and just keep the comma where a semicolon is called for (this is the "splice comma" John Updike is accused of), and when the wrong joining words are used. The splice comma first.

> It was the Queen's birthday on Saturday, she got a lot of presents.
> Jim woke up in an unfamiliar bed, he felt lousy.

Now, so many highly respected writers adopt the splice comma that a rather unfair rule emerges on this one: only do it if you're famous. Samuel Beckett spliced his way merrily through such novels as *Molloy* and *Malone Dies*, thumbing his nose at the semicolon all the way: "There I am then, he leaves me, he's in a hurry." But then Beckett was not only a genius, he was a man who wrote in French when he didn't have to; we can surely agree he earned the right to be ungrammatical if he felt like it. Besides, he is not alone. E. M. Forster did it; Somerset Maugham did it; the list is endless. Done knowingly by an established writer, the comma splice is effective, poetic, dashing. Done equally knowingly by people who are not published writers, it can look weak or presumptuous. Done ignorantly by ignorant people, it is awful.

Meanwhile, words that must not be used to join two sentences together with a comma are *however* and *nevertheless*, as in, "It was the Queen's birthday on Saturday, nevertheless, she had no post whatever"; "Jim woke up in his own bed, however, he felt great." Again, the requirement is for either a new sentence or one of those unpopular semicolons.

It was the Queen's birthday on Saturday;
  nevertheless, she had no post whatever.
Jim woke up in his own bed; however,
  he felt great.

3. Commas filling gaps

Are we halfway yet? I hope so, but I doubt it. Anyway, this one is quite simple, involving missing words cunningly implied by a comma:

Annie had dark hair; Sally, fair.

This doesn't arise very much these days, though, does it? I wonder why?

4. Commas before direct speech

This usage is likely to lapse. Many writers prefer to use colons; others just open the inverted commas — a pretty unambiguous sign that direct speech is coming. Personally, I seem to ring the changes. Since this is a genuine old pause-for-breath use of the comma, however, it would be a shame to see it go.

> The Queen said, "Doesn't anyone know it's my birthday?"

5. Commas setting off interjections

Blimey, what would we do without it? Stop, or I'll scream.

6. Commas that come in pairs

This is where comma usage all starts getting tricky. The first rule of bracketing commas is that you use them to mark both ends of a "weak interruption" to a sentence — or a piece of "additional information". The commas mark the places where the reader can — as it were — place an elegant two-pronged fork and cleanly lift out a section of the sentence, leaving no obvious damage to the whole. Thus:

> John Keats, who never did any harm to anyone, is often invoked by grammarians.
> I am, of course, going steadily nuts.
> *Nicholas Nickleby*, published in 1839, uses a great many commas.
> The Queen, who has double the number of birthdays of most people, celebrated yet another birthday.

In all these cases, the bits between the commas can be removed, leaving the sentence arguably less interesting, but grammatically entire.

As with other paired bracketing devices (such as parentheses, dashes and quotation marks), there is actual mental cruelty involved, incidentally, in opening up a pair of commas and then neglecting to deliver the closing one. The reader hears the first shoe drop and then strains in agony to hear the second. In dramatic terms, it's like putting a gun on the mantelpiece in Act I and then having the heroine drown herself quietly offstage in the bath during the interval. It's just not cricket. Take the example, "The Highland Terrier is the cutest, and perhaps the best of all dog species." Sensitive people trained to listen for the second comma (after "best") find themselves quite stranded by that kind of thing. They feel cheated and giddy. In very bad cases, they fall over.

However, why is it that sometimes these pairs of commas are incorrect? One *Telegraph* correspondent wrote to complain about a frequent newspaper solecism, and the example he gave was, "The leading stage director, Nicholas Hytner, has been appointed to the Royal National Theatre." Shouldn't the commas be removed in cases such as this, he asked? Well, yes. Absolutely. For a start, if you removed the name "Nicholas Hytner" from this particular sentence, it would make no sense at all. But there is a larger grammatical point here, too. Consider the difference between:

The people in the queue who managed to get tickets were very satisfied.

and:

The people in the queue, who managed to get tickets, were very satisfied.

In the first case, the reader infers from the
absence of commas that not everyone in
the queue was fortunate. Some people did
not get tickets. (The ones who did were,
naturally, cock-a-hoop.) In the second version everyone in the queue gets tickets,
hurrah, and I just hope it turned out to be
for something nice. The issue here is
whether the bit between the commas is
"defining" or not. If the clause is "defining", you don't need to present it with a
pair of commas. Thus:

The Highland Terriers that live in our
street aren't cute at all.

If the information in the clause is "non-
defining", however, then you do:

The Highland Terriers, when they are
barking, are a nightmare.

Now, here's a funny thing. When the interruption to the sentence comes at the beginning or at the end, the grammatical rule of
commas-in-pairs still applies, *even if you can*

only see one of them. Thus:

> Of course, there weren't enough tickets to go round.

is, from the grammatical point of view, the same as:

> There weren't, of course, enough tickets to go round.

as well as:

> There weren't enough tickets to go round, of course.

In many cases nowadays, the commas bracketing so-called weak interruptions are becoming optional. And I say three cheers for that, quite frankly. Where I get into a tangle with copy-editors is with sentences such as:

> Belinda opened the trap door, and after listening for a minute she closed it again.

This is, actually, all right. True, it isn't elegant, but it uses the comma grammatically as a "joining" comma, before the "and". Most editors, however, turn purple at the

sight of such a sentence. It becomes, suddenly:

> Belinda opened the trap door and,
> after listening for a minute, closed it
> again.

It seems to me that there are two proper uses
of the comma in conflict here, and that the
problem arises simply from the laudable in-
stinct in both the writer and the editor to
choose *just one use at a time*. In previous centuries — as we can see in those examples
from Fielding and Dickens — every single
use of the comma would be observed:

> Belinda opened the trap door, and,
> after listening for a minute, she
> closed it again.

Nowadays the fashion is against grammatical fussiness. A passage peppered with
commas — which in the past would have indicated painstaking and authoritative editorial attention — smacks simply of no back-
bone. People who put in all the commas be-
tray themselves as moral weaklings with
empty lives and out-of-date reference books.
Back at *The New Yorker*, Thurber tells the
story of "the grison anecdote" — a story

about a soap salesman who belatedly spots a grison (a South American weasel-like carnivore) on a porch in New Jersey. Now, Thurber says he commanded Ross not to change a word of this piece, but he was obviously asking for trouble. "It preserves the fine texture of the most delicate skin and lends a lasting and radiant rosiness to the complexion my God what *is* that thing?" says the salesman. Ross, of course, inserted a comma after "my God". He just couldn't help himself.

,

The big final rule for the comma is one that you won't find in any books by grammarians. It is quite easy to remember, however. The rule is: don't use commas like a stupid person. I mean it. More than any other mark, the comma requires the writer to use intelligent discretion and to be simply alert to potential ambiguity. For example:

1 Leonora walked on her head, a little higher than usual.
2 The driver managed to escape from the vehicle before it sank and swam to the river-bank.
3 Don't guess, use a timer or watch.
4 The convict said the judge is mad.

117

In the first example, of course, the comma has been misplaced and belongs after "on". The second example suggests that the vehicle swam to the river-bank, rather than the passenger. It requires a comma after "sank". The third is pretty interesting, since it actually conveys the opposite of its intended meaning. What it appears to say is, "Don't guess, or use a timer or a watch", when in fact it only wants to tell you not to guess. It therefore requires a semicolon or even a full stop after "guess", rather than a comma. The fourth makes perfect sense, of course — unless what's intended is: "The convict, said the judge, is mad."

Two particular stupid uses of the comma are proliferating and need to be noted. One is the comma memorably described in the "This English" column of the *New Statesman* in the late 1970s as "the yob's comma": "The yob's comma, of course, has no syntactical value: it is the equivalent of a fuddled gasp for breath, as the poor writer marshals his battered thoughts." Examples cited in the *New Statesman* included this, from *The Guardian*:

The society decided not to prosecute the owners of the Windsor Safari Park, where animals, have allegedly been fed live to snakes and lions, on legal advice.

The comma after "animals" is not only ungrammatical and intrusive, but throws the end of the sentence ("on legal advice") into complete semantic chaos. Meanwhile, moronic sentences such as "Parents, are being urged to take advantage of a scheme designed to prevent children getting lost in supermarkets" and "What was different back then, was if you disagreed with the wrong group, you could end up with no head!" are observably on the increase.

Less stoppable is the drift towards American telegraphese in news headlines, where the comma is increasingly given the job of replacing the word "and". Thus:

UK study spurns al-Qaeda, Iraq link
Mother, three sons die in farm fire

,

So that's nearly it for the comma. Although it is not true that the legal profession has historically eschewed commas altogether, one begins to realise there is a sensible reason for its traditional wariness. It is sometimes said, for instance, that Sir Roger Casement (1864–1916), the Irish would-be insurrectionist, was actually "hanged on a comma", which you have to admit sounds like a bit of very rough justice, though jolly intriguing. How do you get hanged on a comma, exactly? Doesn't the rope keep slipping off? Well, having landed in Ireland in 1916 from a German submarine, Casement was arrested and charged under the Treason Act of 1351, whereupon his defence counsel opted to argue a point of punctuation — which is the last refuge of the scoundrel, of course; but never mind, you can't blame the chap, it must have seemed worth a go. His point was that the Treason Act was not only written in Norman French but was unpunctuated, and was thus open to interpretation. The contested words in question, translated literally, were:

If a man be adherent to the king's enemies in his realm giving to them aid and comfort in the realm or elsewhere . . .

Casement's defence argued that, since Casement had not been adherent to the king's enemies "in the realm" (indeed, on the contrary, had scrupulously conducted all his treasonous plotting abroad), he was not guilty. Now, I guarantee you can look at this set of words for hours at a stretch without seeing any virtue in this pathetic contention. Casement was clearly condemned by the phrase "or elsewhere", regardless of how you punctuate it. However, two judges duly traipsed off to the Public Record Office to examine the original statute and discovered under a microscope a faint but helpful *virgule* after the second "realm" which apparently (don't ask) cleared up the whole thing. Mr Justice Darling ruled that "giving aid and comfort to the king's enemies" were words of apposition:

> They are words to explain what is meant by being adherent to, and we think that if a man be adherent to the king's enemies elsewhere, he is equally adherent to the king's enemies, and if he is adherent to the king's enemies, then he commits the treason which the statute of Edward III defines.

How this story ever got the sensational name "hanged on a comma", however, is an interesting matter. "Tried to get off on a comma" is a more accurate representation of the truth.

A similar comma dispute still rages today, in a case with less explosive overtones. On his deathbed in April 1991, Graham Greene corrected and signed a typed document which restricts access to his papers at Georgetown University. *Or does it?* The document, before correction, stated:

> I, Graham Greene, grant permission to Norman Sherry, my authorised biographer, excluding any other to quote from my copyright material published or unpublished.

Being a chap who had corrected proofs all his life, Greene automatically added a comma after "excluding any other" and died the next day without explaining what he intended by it. And a great ambiguity was thereby created. Are all other researchers excluded from quoting the material? Or only other biographers? The librarian at Georgetown interprets the document to mean that nobody besides Norman Sherry can consult the material at all. Meanwhile others, including Greene's son, argue that the comma was carefully inserted by Greene only to indicate that Sherry was the sole authorised biographer.

It is worth pointing out here, by the way, that legal English, with its hifalutin efforts to cover everything, nearly always ends up leaving itself semantically wide open like this, and that if Greene had been allowed to write either "Let Norman Sherry see the stuff and no one else" or, "Don't let other biographers quote from it, but otherwise all are welcome", none of this ridiculous palaver would have transpired.

Airs and Graces

When I was about fourteen years old, a friend at school who spent the summer holidays in Michigan set me up with an American pen-pal. This is not an episode I am proud to remember. In fact, one day I hope to be able to forget it: the ensuing correspondence, after all, ran to only three pages, and no one from the Oxford University Press has, as yet, suggested collecting it in book form with scholarly apparatus and footnotes. But for the time being I need to get it off my chest, so here it is. The trouble was, Kerry-Anne was an everyday teenager with no literary pretensions — and for some reason this made the precocious blue-stocking in me feverishly uncomfortable. When her first letter arrived (she had pluckily set the ball rolling) I was absolutely appalled. It was in huge handwriting, like an infant's. It was on pink paper, with carefree spelling errors — and where the dots over the I's ought to be, there were *bubbles*. "I am strawberry blonde," she wrote, "with a light dusting of freckles." In hindsight I see it was unrealistic to expect a pen-pal from the 8th grade in Detroit to write like Samuel Johnson. But on the other hand, what earthly use to me was this vapid mousey moron parading a pigmentational handicap?

To this day I am ashamed of what I did to Kerry-Anne (who unsurprisingly never wrote back). I replied to her childish letter on grown-up deckled green paper with a fountain pen. Whether I actually donned a velvet smoking jacket for the occasion I can't remember, but I know I deliberately dropped the word "desultory", and I think I may even have used some French. Pretentious? Well, to adapt Gustave Flaubert's famous identification with Emma Bovary, *"Adrian Mole, âgé de treize ans et trois quarts . . . c'est moi."* The main reason I recall this shameful teenage epiphany, however, is that in my mission to blast little Kerry-Anne out of the water, I pulled out (literally) all the stops: I used a semicolon. "I watch television in a desultory kind of way; I find there is not much on," I wrote. And it felt so good, you know. It felt fantastic. It was like that bit in Crocodile Dundee when our rugged hero scoffs at the switchblade of his would-be mugger, and produces a foot-long weapon of his own, "Call that a knife? THAT's a KNIFE."

In this chapter I want to examine punctuation as an art. Naturally, therefore, this is where the colon and semicolon waltz in together, to a big cheer from all the writers in the audience. Just look at those glamorous punctuation marks twirling in the lights from the glitter-ball: are they not beautiful? Are they not graceful? Ask professional writers about punctuation and they will not start striking the board about the misuse of the apostrophe; instead they will jabber in a rather breathless manner about the fate of the semicolon. Is it endangered? What will we do if it disappears? Have you noticed that newspapers use it less and less? Save the semicolon! It is essential to our craft! But their strength of attachment is justified. Taking the marks we have examined so far, is there any art involved in using the apostrophe? No. Using the apostrophe correctly is a mere negative proof: it tells the world you are not a thicko. The comma, while less subject to universal rules, is still a utilitarian mark, racing about with its ears back, trying to serve both the sense and the sound of the sentence — and of course wearing itself to a frazzle for a modest bowl of Chum. Using the comma well announces that you have an ear for sense and rhythm, confidence in your style and a proper respect for your reader, but it does not mark you out as a master of your craft.

But colons and semicolons — well, they are in a different league, my dear! They give such lift! Assuming a sentence rises into the air with the initial capital letter and lands with a soft-ish bump at the full stop, the humble comma can keep the sentence aloft all right, like this, UP, for hours if necessary, UP, like this, UP, sort-of bouncing, and then falling down, and then UP it goes again, assuming you have enough additional things to say, although in the end you may run out of ideas and then you have to roll along the ground with no commas at all until some sort of surface resistance takes over and you run out of steam anyway and then eventually with the help of three dots . . . you stop. But the thermals that benignly waft our sentences to new altitudes — that allow us to coast on air, and loop-the-loop, suspending the laws of gravity — well, they are the colons and semicolons. If you don't believe me, ask Virginia Woolf:

As for the other experiences, the solitary ones, which people go through alone, in their bedrooms, in their offices, walking the fields and the streets of London, he had them; had left home, a mere boy, because of his mother; she lied; because he came down to tea for the fiftieth time with his hands unwashed; because he could see no future for a poet in Stroud; and so, making a confidant of his little sister, had gone to London leaving an absurd note behind him, such as great men have written, and the world has read later when the story of their struggles has become famous.

Virginia Woolf, *Mrs Dalloway*, 1925

Look at that sentence fly. Amazing. The way it stays up like that. Would anyone mind if I ate the last sandwich?

Of course, nothing is straightforward in the world of literary taste. Just as there are writers who worship the semicolon, there are other high stylists who dismiss it — who label it, if you please, middle-class. James Joyce preferred the colon, as more authentically classical; P. G. Wodehouse did an effortlessly marvellous job without it; George Orwell tried to avoid the semicolon completely in *Coming Up for Air* (1939), telling his editor in 1947, "I had decided about this time that the semicolon is an unnecessary stop and that I would write my next book without one." Martin Amis included just one semicolon in *Money* (1984), and was afterwards (more than usually) pleased with himself. The American writer Donald Barthelme wrote that the semicolon is "ugly, ugly as a tick on a dog's belly". Fay Weldon says she positively dislikes semicolons, "which is odd, because I don't dislike anybody really". Meanwhile, that energetic enemy to all punctuation Gertrude Stein (remember she said the comma was "servile"?) said that semicolons suppose themselves superior to the comma, but are mistaken:

> They are more powerful more imposing more pretentious than a comma but they are a comma all the same. They really have within them deeply within them fundamentally within them the comma nature.
> Gertrude Stein,
> "Poetry and Grammar", 1935

But how much notice should we take of those pompous sillies who denounce the semicolon? I say, none at all. I say they are just show-offs. And I say it's wonderful that when Umberto Eco was congratulated by an academic reader for using no semi-colons in *The Name of the Rose* (1983) he cheerfully explained (so the apocryphal story goes) that the machine he typed *The Name of the Rose* on simply didn't have a semicolon, so it was slightly unwise of this earnest chap to make too much of it.

Non-writers are wary of both the colon and the semicolon, though, partly because all this rarefied debate rages above their heads. Eric Partridge, in his 1953 book *You Have a Point There*, says that using colons in your writing is the equivalent of playing the piano with crossed hands. But sadly, anyone lazily looking for an excuse not to master the colon and semicolon can always locate a respectable reason, because so many are advanced. Here are some of the most common:

1 They are old-fashioned
2 They are middle-class
3 They are optional
4 They are mysteriously connected to pausing
5 They are dangerously addictive (*vide* Virginia Woolf)
6 The difference between them is too negligible to be grasped by the brain of man

I hope we shall happily demolish all these objections in the following pages. But it is worth remarking that Fleet Street style gurus fly the flag for most of the prejudices listed above — especially as applied to the semicolon, a mark they increasingly strike out with puritanical gusto. The semicolon has currently fallen out of fashion with newspapers, the official reason being that readers of newsprint prefer their sentences short, their paragraphs bite-sized and their columns of type uncluttered by wormy squiggles. It's more likely that the real reasons are a pathetic editorial confusion about usage and a policy of distrusting contributors even when they demonstrably know their onions. But heigh-ho. There is no point trying to turn the clock back. The great theatre critic James Agate, in his diary for 1935, recorded how a notoriously fastidious fellow journalist "once telephoned a semicolon from Moscow". Well. You could imagine the reception he would get today.

;

Are the colon and semicolon old-fashioned? No, but they are *old*. The first printed semicolon was the work of good old Aldus Manutius just two years after

Columbus sailed to the New World, and at the same date and place as the invention of double-entry book-keeping. But although I still swoon every time I look at this particular semicolon from 1494, it was not, as it turns out, the first time a human being ever balanced a dot on top of a comma. The medieval scribes had used a symbol very similar to our modern semicolon in their Latin transcripts to indicate abbreviations (thus "atque" might appear as "atq;"). The Greeks used the semicolon mark to indicate a question (and still do, those crazy guys). Meanwhile, a suspiciously similar mark (the *punctus versus*) was used by medieval scribes to indicate a termination in a psalm. But let's face it, we are not really interested in those dusty old medieval monks. What really concerns us is that, while both the colon and the semicolon had been adopted into English well before 1700, confusion has surrounded their use ever since, and it is really only in the past few decades that grammarians have worked out a clear and satisfactory system for their application — tragically, at precisely the time when modern technological communication threatens to wipe out the subtleties of punctuation altogether.

For many years grammarians were a bit cagey about the difference between the colon and semicolon. Perhaps the colon was more "literary" than the semicolon? One grammarian, writing in 1829, lamented the two marks as "primeval sources of improfitable contention". By and large, however, it was decided that the way to satisfy the punters was to classify the marks hierarchically, in terms of weight. Thus the comma is the lightest mark, then the semicolon, then the colon, then the full stop. Cecil Hartley, in his *Principles of Punctuation: or, The Art of Pointing* (1818), includes this little poem, which tells us the simple one-two-three of punctuation values.

> The stops point out, with truth, the time of pause
> A sentence doth require at ev'ry clause.
> At ev'ry comma, stop while *one* you count;
> At semicolon, *two* is the amount;
> A colon doth require the time of *three;*
> The period *four,* as learned men agree.

This system of sorting punctuation marks as if they were musical rests of ascending value has gone unquestioned for a long time, but do you know what I think? I think it's rubbish. Complete nonsense. Who counts to two? Who counts to three? Imagine all those poor devils who have, abiding by this ridiculous rule, sat at desks for the past three centuries, tapping pencils and trying to work out whether "To err is human, *tap, tap*, to forgive divine" is superior to "To err is human, *tap, tap, TAP*, to forgive divine" — before bursting into tears because each version sounds as bad as the other. The idea of the semicolon as an imperceptible bit weightier than a comma, and the colon as a teensy bit lighter than a full stop, is a wrong-headed way of both characterising the colon and semicolon, and (especially) sorting them out. They are not like so many bags of sugar attached to the belt of a sentence to slow it down. Quite the opposite. Here is the American essayist Lewis Thomas on the semicolon:

The semicolon tells you that there is still some question about the preceding full sentence; something needs to be added [. . .] The period [or full stop] tells you that that is that; if you didn't get all the meaning you wanted or expected, anyway you got all the writer intended to parcel out and now you have to move along. But with the semicolon there you get a pleasant feeling of expectancy; there is more to come; read on; it will get clearer.

The Medusa and the Snail, 1979

Expectation is what these stops are about; expectation and elastic energy. Like internal springs, they propel you forward in a sentence towards more information, and the essential difference between them is that while the semicolon lightly propels you in any direction related to the foregoing ("Whee! Surprise me!"), the colon nudges you along lines already subtly laid down. How can such useful marks be optional, for heaven's sake? As for the other thing, if they are middle-class, I'm a serviette. Of the objections to the colon and semicolon listed above, there is only one I am prepared to concede: that semicolons are dangerously habit-forming. Many writers hooked on semicolons become an embarrassment to their families and friends. Their agents gently remind them, "George Orwell managed without, you know. And look what happened to Marcel Proust: carry on like this and you're only one step away from a cork-lined room!" But the writers rock back and forth on their office chairs, softly tapping the semicolon key and emitting low whimpers. I hear there are now Knightsbridge clinics offering semicolonic irrigation — but for many it may be too late. In her autobiographical *Giving Up the Ghost* (2003), Hilary Mantel reveals: "I have always been addicted to something or other, usually something there's no support group for. Semicolons, for instance, I can never give up for more than two hundred words at a time."

So how should you use the colon, to begin with? H. W. Fowler said that the colon "delivers the goods that have been invoiced in the preceding words", which is not a bad image to start with. But the holy text of the colon and semicolon is the letter written by George Bernard Shaw to T. E. Lawrence in 1924, ticking him off for his over-use of colons in the manuscript of *Seven Pillars of Wisdom*. This superb missive starts with the peremptory, "My dear Luruns [*sic*], Confound you and your book: you are no more to be trusted with a pen than a child with a torpedo" — and then gets even more offensive and hilarious as it goes on. Shaw explains that, having worked out his own system for colons and semicolons, he has checked it against the Bible, and seen that the Bible almost got it right. With such authority behind him, he is offended by Lawrence's cavalier attitude. "I save up the colon jealously for certain effects that no other stop produces," he explains. "As you have no rules, and sometimes throw colons about with an unhinged mind, here are some rules for you."

Shaw is quite famous for his idiosyncratic punctuation. His semicolons, in particular, were his way of making his texts firmly actor-proof — in fact, when Ralph Richardson tried to insert a few dramatic puffs and pants in his opening lines as Bluntschli in a 1931 production of *Arms and the Man* (1894), Shaw stopped him at once and told him to forget the naturalism and observe the punctuation instead. "This is all very well, Richardson," Shaw said (according to Richardson's account), "and it might do for Chekhov, but it doesn't do for me. Your gasps are upsetting my stops and my semicolons, and you've got to stick to them." Richardson said Shaw spoke the truth about this: miss any of Shaw's stops and "the tune won't come off". Look at any Shaw text and you will find both colons and semicolons in overabundance, with deliberate spacing to draw attention to them, too, as if they are genuine musical notation.

Captain Bluntschli. I am very glad to see you ; but you must leave this house at once. My husband has just returned with my future son-in-law ; and they know nothing. If they did, the consequences would be terrible. You are a foreigner : you do not feel our national animosities as we do.

Arms and the Man, Act II

To adopt George Bernard Shaw's use of the semicolon today would obviously be an act of insanity. But in the letter to T. E. Lawrence he is sound on the colon. When two statements are "placed baldly in dramatic apposition", he said, use a colon. Thus, "Luruns could not speak: he was drunk." Shaw explains to Lawrence that when the second statement reaffirms, explains or illustrates the first, you use a colon; also when you desire an abrupt "pull-up": "Luruns was congenitally literary: that is, a liar."

You will see [writes Shaw] that your colons before buts and the like are contraindicated in my scheme, and leave you without anything in reserve for the dramatic occasions mentioned above. You practically do not use semicolons at all. This is a symptom of mental defectiveness, probably induced by camp life.

So the particular strengths of the colon are beginning to become clear. A colon is nearly always preceded by a complete sentence, and in its simplest usage it rather theatrically announces what is to come. Like a well-trained magician's assistant, it pauses slightly to give you time to get a bit worried, and then efficiently whisks away the cloth and reveals the trick complete.

In each of the following examples, incidentally, can't you hear a delighted, satisfied "Yes!" where the colon comes?

This much is clear, Watson: it was the baying of an enormous hound.
(*This much is clear, Watson — yes! it was the baying of an enormous hound.*)
Tom has only one rule in life: never eat anything bigger than your head.
(*Tom had only one rule in life — yes! never eat anything bigger than your head.*)
I pulled out all the stops with Kerry-

Anne: I used a semicolon.
(I pulled out all the stops with Kerry-Anne — yes! I used a semicolon.)

But the "annunciatory" colon is only one variety. As well as the "Yes!" type colon, there is the "Ah" type, when the colon reminds us there is probably more to the initial statement than has met the eye:

I loved Opal Fruits as a child: no one else did.
(I loved Opal Fruits — ah, but nobody else did.)
You can do it: and you will do it.
(You can do it — ah, and you will do it.)

A classic use of the colon is as a kind fulcrum between two antithetical or oppositional statements:

Man proposes: God disposes.

And as Shaw put it so well, the colon can simply pull up the reader for a nice surprise:

I find fault with only three things in this story of yours, Jenkins: the beginning, the middle and the end.

So colons introduce the part of a sentence that exemplifies, restates, elaborates, undermines, explains or balances the preceding part. They also have several formal introductory roles. They start lists (especially lists using semicolons):

> In later life, Kerry-Anne found there were three qualities she disliked in other people: Britishness; superior airs; and a feigned lack of interest in her dusting of freckles.

They set off book and film sub-titles from the main titles:

> Berks and Wankers: a pessimist's view of language preservation
> Gandhi II: The Mahatma Strikes Back

Conventionally, they separate dramatic characters from dialogue:

> PHILIP: Kerry-Anne! Hold still! You've got some gunk on your face!
> KERRY-ANNE: They're *freckles*, Philip. How many more times?

They also start off long quotations and (of course) introduce examples in books on punctuation. What a useful chap the colon is, after all. Forget about counting to three, that's all I ask.

,

So when do you use a semicolon? As we learned in the comma chapter, the main place for putting a semicolon if you are not John Updike is between two related sentences where there is no conjunction such as "and" or "but", and where a comma would be ungrammatical:

I loved Opal Fruits; they are now called Starburst, of course.
It was the baying of an enormous hound; it came from over there!
I remember him when he couldn't write his own name on a gate; now he's Prime Minister.

What the semicolon's anxious supporters fret about is the tendency of contemporary writers to use a dash instead of a semicolon and thus precipitate the end of the world. Are they being alarmist? In each of the examples above, a dash could certainly be substituted for the semicolon without much damage to the sentence. The dash is less formal than the semicolon, which makes it more attractive; it enhances conversational tone; and, as we shall see in the next chapter, it is capable of quite subtle effects. The main reason people use it, however, is that they know *you can't use it wrongly* — which, for a punctuation mark, is an uncommon virtue. But it is worth learning the different effects created by the semicolon and the dash. Whereas the semicolon suggests a connection between the two halves of each of these sentences, the dash ought to be preserved for occasions when the connection is a lot less direct, when it can act as a bridge between bits of fractured sense:

> I loved Opal Fruits — why did they call them Starburst? — reminds me of that joke "What did Zimbabwe used to be called? — Rhodesia. What did Iceland used to be called? — Bejam!"

So it is true that we must keep an eye on the dash — and also the ellipsis (. . .), which is turning up increasingly in emails as shorthand for "more to come, actually . . . it might be related to what I've just written . . . but the main thing is I haven't finished . . . let's just wait and see . . . I could go on like this for hours . . ." However, so long as there remain sentences on this earth that begin with capital letters and end with full stops, there will be a place for the semicolon. True, its use is never obligatory, because a full stop ought always to be an alternative. But that only makes it the more wonderful.

> Popotakis had tried a cinema, a dance hall, baccarat, and miniature golf; now he had four ping-pong tables. He had made good money, for the smart set of Jacksonburg were always hard put to get through the rainy season; the polyglot professional class had made it their rendezvous; even attachés from the legislations and younger members of the Jackson family had come there.
>
> Evelyn Waugh, *Scoop*, 1938

The semicolon has been rightly called "a compliment from the writer to the reader". And a mighty compliment it is, too. The sub-text of a semicolon is, "Now this is a hint. The elements of this sentence, although grammatically distinct, are actually elements of a single notion. I can make it plainer for you — but hey! You're a reader! I don't need to draw you a map!" By the same token, however, an over-reliance on semicolons — to give an air of authorial intention to half-formed ideas thrown together on the page — is rather more of a compliment than some of us care to receive. The American writer Paul Robinson, in his essay "The Philosophy of Punctuation" (2002), says that "pretentious and over-active" semicolons have reached epidemic proportions in the world of academe, where they are used to gloss over imprecise thought. "They place two clauses in some kind of relation to one another but *relieve the writer of saying exactly what that relation is.*" Those are my italics, by the way — but it does sound as if Robinson is a bit worked up. "The semicolon has become so hateful to me," he says in all seriousness, "that I feel almost morally compromised when I use it."

There are times, however, when the semicolon is indispensable in another capacity: when it performs the duties of a kind of Special Policeman in the event of comma fights. If there is one lesson to be learned from this book, it is that there is never a dull moment in the world of punctuation. One minute the semicolon is gracefully joining sentences together in a flattering manner (and sullying Mr Robinson), and the next it is calling a bunch of brawling commas to attention.

> Fares were offered to Corfu, the Greek island, Morocco, Elba, in the Mediterranean, and Paris. Margaret thought about it. She had been to Elba once and had found it dull, to Morocco, and found it too colourful.

There is no option for an upstanding semicolon in such circumstances other than to step in, blow a whistle and restore order.

> Fares were offered to Corfu, the Greek island; Morocco; Elba, in the Mediterranean; and Paris. Margaret thought about it. She had been to Elba once and had found it dull; to Morocco, and found it too colourful.

That's much clearer. And we have *you* to thank, Special Policeman Semicolon. There are two dangers, however, associated with this quell-the-rampant-comma use. One is that, having embarked on a series of clarifying semicolons, the writer loses interest, or forgets, and lapses into a comma (ho ho). The other danger is that weak-charactered writers will be encouraged to ignore the rule that only full sentences should be joined by the semicolon. Sometimes — and I've never admitted this to anyone before — I adopt a kind of stream-of-consciousness sentence structure; somewhat like Virginia Woolf; without full sentences; but it feels OK to do this; rather worrying.

Let us come swiftly to the last proper use of the semicolon. As we discovered in the comma chapter, it is wrong to write, "He woke up in his own bed, however, he felt fine." Linking words such as "however", "nevertheless", "also", "consequently" and "hence" require a semicolon — and, I have to say, this seems pretty self-evident to me. Much as I decry the old count-to-two system, there is an obvious take-a-breath thing going on here. When you read the sentence, "He woke up in his own bed, and he felt fine", you don't draw breath before the "and". You rattle on. Whereas when you read, "He woke up in his own bed; nevertheless, he was OK", an inhalation is surely automatic.

,

It should come as no surprise that writers take an interest in punctuation. I have been told that the dying words of one famous 20th-century writer were, "I should have used fewer semicolons" — and although I have spent months fruitlessly trying to track down the chap responsible, I believe it none the less. If it turns out that no one actually did say this on their death-bed, I shall certainly save it up for my own.

What you have to remember about our punctuation system is that it is very limited. Writers jealous of their individual style are obliged to wring the utmost effect from a tiny range of marks — which explains why they get so desperate when their choices are challenged (or corrected) by copy-editors legislating according to a "house style". You write the words "apple tree" and discover that house style is "apple-tree". This hurts. The alteration seems simply perverse. And no one is immune. When Salman Rushdie's story "Free Radio" (in his book *East, West* [1994]) was first published by *Atlantic Monthly*, I have heard that the magazine repunctuated its deliberately "logorrhoeic" narration without consulting him, presumably on the assumption that punctuation was something Rushdie was happy to leave to others, like the hoovering. Nicholson Baker, in an essay on the history of punctuation in his book *The Size of Thoughts*

(1996), relates an emotional battle with his copy-editor over whether "pantyhose" (as written) should be altered to "panty hose". Baker, incidentally, advocates the return of compound punctuation, such as commas with dashes (, —), semicolons with dashes (; —) and colons with dashes (: —); and in his book *Room Temperature* (1990), muses so poetically on the shape of the comma ("it recalled the pedals of grand pianos, mosquito larvae, paisleys, adult nostril openings, the spiralling decays of fundamental particles, the prows of gondolas . . .") that — well, you've never heard anything like it.

,

See how the sense changes with the punctuation in this example:

Tom locked himself in the shed. England lost to Argentina.

These two statements, as they stand, could be quite unrelated. They merely tell you two things have happened, in the past tense.

Tom locked himself in the shed; England lost to Argentina.

We can infer from the semicolon that these events occurred at the same time, although it is possible that Tom locked himself in the shed because he couldn't bear to watch the match and therefore still doesn't know the outcome. With the semicolon in place, Tom locking himself in the shed and England losing to Argentina sound like two things that really got on the nerves of someone else. "It was a terrible day, Mum: Tom locked himself in the shed; England lost to Argentina; the rabbit electrocuted itself by biting into the power cable of the washing machine."

Tom locked himself in the shed: England lost to Argentina.

All is now clear. Tom locked himself in the shed *because* England lost to Argentina. And who can blame him, that's what I say.

It is sad to think people are no longer learning how to use the colon and semicolon, not least because, in this supreme QWERTY keyboard era, the little finger of the human right hand, deprived of its traditional function, may eventually dwindle and drop off from disuse. But the main reason is that, as Joseph Robertson wrote in an essay on punctuation in 1785, "The

art of punctuation is of infinite consequence in writing; as it contributes to the
perspicuity, and consequently to the
beauty, of every composition." Perspicuity
and beauty of composition are not to be
sneezed at in this rotten world. If colons
and semicolons give themselves airs and
graces, at least they also confer airs and
graces that the language would be lost
without.

Cutting a Dash

In 1885, Anton Chekhov wrote a Christmas short story called "The Exclamation Mark". In this light parody of *A Christmas Carol*, a collegiate secretary named Perekladin has a sleepless night on Christmas Eve after someone at a party offends him — by casting aspersions on his ability to punctuate in an educated way. I know this doesn't sound too promising, but stick with it, it's Chekhov, and the general rule is that you can't go wrong with Chekhov. At this party, the rattled Perekladin insists that, despite his lack of a university education, forty years' practice has taught him how to use punctuation, thank you very much. But that night, after he goes to bed, he is troubled; and then he is haunted. Scrooge-like, he is visited on this momentous Christmas Eve by a succession of spectres, which teach him a lesson he will never forget.

And what are these spectres? They are all punctuation marks. Yes, this really is a story about punctuation — and first to disturb Perekladin's sleep is a crowd of fiery, flying commas, which Perekladin banishes by repeating the rules he knows for using them. Then come full stops; colons and semicolons; question marks. Again, he keeps his head and sends them away. But then a question mark unbends itself, straightens up — and Perekladin realises he is stumped. In forty years he has had no reason to use an exclamation mark! He has no idea what it is for. The inference for the reader is clear: nothing of any emotional significance has ever happened to Perekladin. Nothing relating, in any case, to the "delight, indignation, joy, rage and other feelings" an exclamation mark is in the business of denoting.

As epiphanies go, this isn't quite the same as seeing Tiny Tim's ownerless crutch propped in the inglenook, but Perekladin is affected none the less.

> The poor pen-pusher felt cold and ill at ease, as if he had caught typhus. The exclamation mark was no longer standing behind his closed eyes but in front of him, in the room, by his wife's dressing-table, and it was winking at him mockingly.
>
> Translation:
> Harvey Pitcher in Chekhov,
> *The Comic Stories*, 1998

What can poor Perekladin do? When he hails a cab on Christmas Day, he spots immediately that the driver is an exclamation mark. Things are getting out of hand. At the home of his "chief", the doorman is another exclamation mark. It is time to take a stand — and, signing himself into the visitors' book at his chief's house, Perekladin suddenly sees the way. Defiantly he writes his name, "Collegiate Secretary Yefim Perekladin" and adds three exclamation marks, "!!!"

And as he wrote those three marks, he felt delight and indignation, he was joyful and he seethed with rage.
"Take that, take that!" he muttered, pressing down hard on the pen.

And the phantom exclamation mark disappears.
Most of us can't remember a time before we learned to punctuate. We perhaps remember learning to read and to spell, but not the moment when we found out that adding the symbol "!" to a sentence somehow changed the tone of voice it was read in. Luckily we are taught such stuff when we are young enough not to ask awkward questions, because the way this

symbol "!" turns "I can't believe it" into "I can't believe it!" is the sort of dizzying convention that requires to be taken absolutely on trust. Of my own exclamation-mark history (which is not one to be proud of) all I can clearly recollect of its early days is that the standard keyboard of a manual typewriter in the 1970s — on which I did my first typing — did not offer an exclamation mark. You had to type a full stop, then back-space and type an apostrophe on top of it. Quite a deterrent to expressive punctuation, Mister Remington. But in fact, of course, all one's resourceful back-space/shift-key efforts only added to the satisfaction of seeing the emphatic little black blighter sitting cheerfully on the page.

This chapter is about expressive, attention-seeking punctuation — punctuation that cuts a dash; punctuation that can't help saying it with knobs on, such as the exclamation mark, the dash, the italic. Of course the effect of such marks can be over-relied on; of course they are condemned by Gertrude Stein (strange woman). Yet I can't help thinking, in its defence, that our system of punctuation is limited enough already without us dismissing half of it as rubbish. I say we should remember the fine example of

Perekladin, who found catharsis in an exclamation mark, and also of the French 19th-century novelist Victor Hugo, who — when he wanted to know how *Les Misérables* was selling — reportedly telegraphed his publisher with the simple inquiry "?" and received the expressive reply "!"

)

Everyone knows the exclamation mark — or exclamation point, as it is known in America. It comes at the end of a sentence, is unignorable and hopelessly heavy-handed, and is known in the newspaper world as a screamer, a gasper, a startler or (sorry) a dog's cock. Here's one! And here's another! In humorous writing, the exclamation mark is the equivalent of canned laughter (F. Scott Fitzgerald — that well-known knockabout gag-man — said it was like laughing at your own jokes), and I can attest there is only one thing more mortifying than having an exclamation mark removed by an editor: an exclamation mark added in.

Despite all the efforts of typewriter manufacturers, you see, the exclamation mark has refused to die out. Introduced by humanist printers in the 15th century, it was known as "the note of admiration" until the mid 17th century, and was defined — in a lavishly titled 1680 book *Treatise of Stops, Points, or Pauses, and of Notes which are used in Writing and Print; Both very necessary to be well known And the Use of each to be carefully taught* — in the following rhyming way:

This stop denotes our Suddain
   Admiration,
Of what we Read, or Write,
   or giv Relation,
And is always cal'd an Exclamation.

Ever since it came along, grammarians have warned us to be wary of the exclamation mark, mainly because, even when we try to muffle it with brackets (!), it still shouts, flashes like neon, and jumps up and down. In the family of punctuation, where the full stop is daddy and the comma is mummy, and the semicolon quietly practises the piano with crossed hands, the exclamation mark is the big attention-deficit brother who gets over-excited and breaks things and laughs too loudly. Traditionally it is used:

1 in involuntary ejaculations: "Phew! Lord love a duck!"

2 to salute or invoke: "O mistress mine! Where are you roaming?"

3 to exclaim (or admire): "How many goodly creatures are there here!"

4 for drama: "That's not the Northern Lights, that's Manderley!"

5 to make a commonplace sentence more emphatic: "I could really do with some Opal Fruits!"

6 to deflect potential misunderstanding of irony: "I don't mean it!"

Personally, I use exclamation marks for email salutations, where I feel a "Dear Jane" is over-formal. "Jane!" I write, although I am beginning to discover this practice is not universally acceptable. I suppose the rule is: only use an exclamation mark when you are absolutely sure you require such a big effect. H. W. Fowler said, "An excessive use of exclamation marks is a certain indication of an unpractised writer or of one who wants to add a spurious dash of sensation to something unsensational." On the other hand, it sometimes seems hurtful to suppress the exclamation mark when — after all — it doesn't mean any harm to anyone, and is so desperately keen.

The question mark, with its elegant sea-horse profile, takes up at least double the space on the page of an exclamation mark, yet gets on people's nerves considerably less. What would we do without it? Like the exclamation mark, it is a development of the full stop, a "terminator", used only at the ends of sentences, starting out as the *punctus interrogativus* in the second half of the 8th century, when it resembled a lightning flash, striking from right to left. The name "question mark" (which is rather a dull one, quite frankly) was acquired in the second half of the 19th century, and has never caught on universally. Journalists dictating copy will call it a "query", and — while we are on the subject of dictation — in this passage from P. G. Wodehouse's *Over Seventy* (1957) it is delightfully called something else:

How anybody can compose a story by word of mouth face to face with a bored-looking secretary with a note-book is more than I can imagine. Yet many authors think nothing of saying, "Ready, Miss Spelvin? Take dictation. Quote No comma Sir Jasper

Murgatroyd comma close quotes comma said no better make it hissed Evangeline comma quote I would not marry you if you were the last man on earth period close quotes Quote Well comma I'm not comma so the point does not arise comma close quotes replied Sir Jasper twirling his moustache cynically period And so the long day wore on period. End of chapter."

If I had to do that sort of thing I should be feeling all the time that the girl was saying to herself as she took it down, "Well comma this beats me period How comma with homes for the feebleminded touting for custom on every side comma has a man like this succeeded in remaining at large mark of interrogation."

Question marks are used when the question is direct:

What is the capital of Belgium?
Have you been there?
Did you find the people very strange?

When the question is inside quotation marks, again it is required:

"Did you try the moules and chips?" he asked.

But when the question is indirect, the sentence manages without it:

What was the point of all this sudden interest in Brussels, he wondered.
I asked if she had something in particular against the Belgian national character.

Increasingly people are (ignorantly) adding question marks to sentences containing indirect questions, which is a bit depressing, but the reason is not hard to find: blame the famous upward inflection caught by all teenage viewers of *Neighbours* in the past twenty years. Previously, people said "you know?" and "know what I'm saying?" at the end of every sentence. Now they don't bother with the words and just use the question marks, to save time. Everything ends up becoming a question? I'm talking about statements? It's getting quite annoying? But at least it keeps the question mark alive so it can't be all bad?

Deciding which way round to print the question mark wasn't as straightforward as you might think, incidentally. In its traditional orientation, with the curve to the right, it appears to cup an ear towards the preceding prose, which seems natural enough, though perhaps only because that's how we are used to seeing it. But people have always played around with it. In the 16th century the printer Henry Denham had the sophisticated idea of reversing the mark when indicating a rhetorical question (to differentiate it from a direct question), but it didn't catch on. You can imagine other printers muttering uncertainly, "Rhetorical question? What's a rhetorical question? Is *this* a rhetorical question?" — and not being able to answer. The Spanish Academy, however, in 1754 ratified the rather marvellous and flamboyant idea of complementing terminal question marks and exclamation marks with upside-down versions at the beginnings, thus:

¡Lord, love a duck!
¿Doesn't Spanish look different from
    everything else now we've done this?

And it's not a bad system at all. Evidently Bill Gates has personally assured the Spanish Academy that he will never allow the upside-down question mark to disappear from Microsoft word-processing programs, which must be reassuring for millions of Spanish-speaking people, though just a piddling afterthought as far as he's concerned. Meanwhile, in Hebrew the question mark is exactly the same as our own, despite the fact that it ought logically to be flipped into reverse, since the words run from right to left. Remember Professor Higgins in *My Fair Lady*: "The Arabs learn Arabian with the speed of summer lightning / The Hebrews learn it backwards, which is absolutely frightening"? So we have an interesting and perverse perceptual problem in Hebrew: with the question mark the same way round as our own, it looks back to front.

Unsurprisingly, Gertrude Stein was not a fan of the question mark. Are you beginning to suspect — as I am — that there was something wrong at home? Anyway, Stein said that of all punctuation marks the question mark was "the most completely uninteresting":

It is evident that if you ask a question you ask a question but anybody who can read at all knows when a question is a question [. . .] I never could bring myself to use a question mark, I always found it positively revolting, and now very few do use it.

Since Stein wrote these remarks in 1935, it's interesting that she thought the question mark was on the way out, even then. Those of us brought up with the question-mark ethic are actually horrified when a direct question is written without a question mark — as in, for example, the film title *Who Framed Roger Rabbit*. Unmarked questions left dangling in this way make me feel like an old-fashioned headmaster waiting for a child to remember his manners. "And?" I keep wanting to say. *"And?"* "Can you spare any old records," it still says in that charity-shop window – only now it's a printed sign, not a handwritten one. Every time I pass it, it drives me nuts. Meanwhile, as Kingsley Amis points out in his *The King's English*, many people start sentences with words such as, "May I crave the hospitality of your columns" and then get so involved in a long sentence that they forget it started as a question, so finish it with a full stop.

To do so not only sends the interested reader, if there is one, back to the start to check that the fellow did at any rate start to ask a direct question, it also carries the disagreeable and perhaps truthful suggestion that the writer thinks a request from the likes of him is probably a needless politeness to the likes of the editor.

What a marvellous little aside, by the way: "if there is one".

,

Of all the conventions of print that make no objective sense, the use of italics is the one that puzzles most. How *does* it work? Yet ever since italic type was invented in the 15th century, it has been customary to mix italic with roman to lift certain words out of the surrounding context and mark them as special. None of the marks in this chapter so far has anything to do with grammar, really. They are all to do with symbolically notating the music of the spoken language: of asking the question "?" and receiving the answer "!" Italics have developed to serve certain purposes for us that we never stop to question. When was the last time you panicked in the face of italics, "Hang on, this writing's gone all wobbly"? Instead we all know that italics are the print equivalent of under-lining, and that they are used for:

1 titles of books, newspapers, albums, films such as (unfortunately) *Who Framed Roger Rabbit*
2 emphasis of certain words
3 foreign words and phrases
4 examples when writing about language

We even accept the mad white-on-black convention that *when a whole sentence is in italics, you use* roman type *to emphasise a key word inside it.* Some British newspapers, notably *The Guardian*, have dropped the use of italics for titles, which as far as I can see makes life a lot more difficult for the reader without any compensating benefits. Like the exclamation mark, however, italics should be used sparingly for the purposes of emphasis — partly because they are a confession of stylistic failure, and partly because readers glancing at a page of type might unconsciously clock the italicised bit before starting their proper work of beginning in the top left-hand corner. Martin Amis, reviewing Iris Murdoch's novel *The Philosopher's Pupil* in *The Observer* in 1983, complained of a narrator, "N", who was irritating on a variety of scores, and explains what can happen to a writer who uses italics too much:

Apart from a weakness for quotation marks, "N" also has a weakness for ellipses, dashes, exclamations and italics, especially italics. Each page is corrugated by half a dozen underlinings, normally a sure sign of stylistic irresolution. A jangled, surreal (and much shorter) version of the book could be obtained by reading the italic type and omitting the roman. It would go something like this:

deep, significant, awful, horrid, sickening, absolutely disgusting, guilt, accuse, secret, conspiracy, go to the cinema, go for a long walk, an entirely different matter, an entirely new way, become a historian, become a philosopher, never sing again, Stella, jealous, happy, cad, bloody fool, God, Christ, mad, crazy . . .

Martin Amis, collected in
The War Against Cliché, 2001

What a rotten thing to do. But on the other hand, I feel he has saved us all the bother of reading the book now.

　　　　　　　　❦

When Amis *fils* mentioned quotation marks as an annoyance in *The Philosopher's Pupil*, he was not objecting to those that indicate actual quotations. Inverted commas (or speech marks, or quotes) are sometimes used by fastidious writers as a kind of linguistic rubber glove, distancing them from vulgar words or clichés they are too refined to use in the normal way. This "N" character in Iris Murdoch's novel evidently can't bring himself to say "keep in touch" without sealing it hygienically within inverted commas, and doubtless additionally indicating his irony with two pairs of curled fingers held up at either side of his face. In newspapers, similar inverted commas are sometimes known as "scare quotes", as when a headline says "BRITAIN BUYS 'WRONG' VACCINE", "ROBERT MAXWELL 'DEAD' ", or "DEAD MAN 'EATEN' IN GRUESOME CAT HORROR". Such inverted commas (usually single, rather than double) are understood by readers to mean that there is some authority for this story, perhaps even a quotable source, but that the newspaper itself won't yet state it as fact. Evidently there is no legal protection provided by such weaselly inverted commas: if you assert someone is 'LYING', it's pretty much the same in law as saying he is lying. And we all know the dead man was definitely eaten by those gruesome cats — otherwise no one would have raised the possibility. The interesting thing is how this practice relates to the advertising of 'PIZZAS' in quite large supermarket chains. To those of us accustomed to newspaper headlines, 'PIZZAS' in inverted commas suggests these *might* be pizzas, but nobody's promising anything, and if they turn out to be cardboard with a bit of cheese on top, you can't say you weren't warned.

There is a huge amount of ignorance concerning the use of quotation marks. A catalogue will advertise that its pineapple ring slicer works just like 'a compass'. Why? Why doesn't it work just like a compass? There is a serious cognitive problem highlighted here, I think; a real misunderstanding of what writing is. Nigel Hall, a reader in literacy education at Manchester Metropolitan University who studies the way children learn to punctuate, told me about one small boy who peppered his work with quotation marks, regardless of whether it was reporting any speech. Why did he do that? "Because it's all me talking," the child explained, and I imagine it was hard to argue against such immaculate logic. It seems to me that the 'PIZZAS' people, who put signs in their windows — 'NOW OPEN SUNDAYS',

'THANK YOU FOR NOT SMOK-ING' — have the same problem as this little boy. If they are saying this thing, announcing it, then they feel that logically they have to present it in speech marks, because *it's all them talking.*

Comfortable though we are with our modern usage, it has taken a long time to evolve, and will of course evolve further, so we mustn't get complacent. Until the beginning of the 18th century, quotation marks were used in England only to call attention to sententious remarks. Then in 1714 someone had the idea of using them to denote direct speech, and by the time of the first edition of Henry Fielding's *Tom Jones* in 1749, inverted commas were used by printers both to contain the speech and to indicate in a general, left-hand marginal way that there was speech going on.

Here the Book dropt from her Hand, and a Shower of Tears ran down into her Bosom. In this Situation she had continued a Minute, when the Door opened, and in came Lord *Fellamar*. *Sophia* started from her Chair at his Entrance ; and his Lordship advancing forwards, and making a low Bow said, ' I am afraid, Miss *Wes-* ' *tern*, I break in upon you abruptly.' ' In-

' deed, my Lord,' says she, ' I must own
' myself a little surprized at this unexpect-
' ed Visit.' ' If this Visit be unexpected,
' Madam,' answered Lord *Fellamar,* ' my
' Eyes must have been very faithless Inter-
' preters of my Heart ... '

Since the 18th century we have stan-
dardised the use of quotation marks — but
only up to a point. Readers are obliged to
get used to the idea from an early age that
"Double or single?" is a question not ap-
plicable only to beds, tennis and cream.
We see both double and single quotation
marks every day, assimilate both, and try
not to think about it. Having been trained
to use double quotation marks for speech,
however, with single quotations for quota-
tions-within-quotations, I grieve to see the
rule applied the other way round. There is
a difference between saying someone is
"out of sorts" (a direct quote) and 'out of
sorts' (i.e., not feeling very well): when
single quotes serve both functions, you
lose this distinction. Also, with the poor
apostrophe already confusing people so
much, a sentence that begins with a single
quote and contains an apostrophe after
three or four words is quite confusing ty-
pographically, because you automatically

assume the apostrophe is the closing quotation mark:

'I was at St Thomas' Hospital,' she said.

There is, too, a gulf between American usage and our own, with Americans always using double quotation marks and American grammarians insisting that, if a sentence ends with a phrase in inverted commas, all the terminal punctuation for the sentence must come tidily inside the speech marks, even when this doesn't seem to make sense.

Sophia asked Lord Fellamar if he was "out of his senses". (British)
Sophia asked Lord Fellamar if he was "out of his senses." (American)

Since where and when to put other punctuation in direct speech is a real bother to some people, here are some basic rules:

When a piece of dialogue is attributed at its end, conclude it with a comma inside the inverted commas:

"You are out of your senses, Lord

Fellamar," gasped Sophia.

When the dialogue is attributed at the start, conclude with a full stop inside the inverted commas:

> Lord Fellamar replied, "Love has so totally deprived me of reason that I am scarce accountable for my actions."

When the dialogue stands on its own, the full stop comes inside the inverted commas:

> "Upon my word, my Lord, I neither understand your words nor your behaviour."

When only a fragment of speech is being quoted, put punctuation outside the inverted commas:

> Sophia recognised in Lord Fellamar the "effects of frenzy", and tried to break away.

When the quotation is a question or exclamation, the terminal marks come inside the inverted commas:

"Am I really to conceive your Lordship to be out of his senses?" cried Sophia.
"Unhand me, sir!" she demanded.

But when the question is posed by the sentence rather than by the speaker, logic demands that the question mark goes outside the inverted commas:

Why didn't Sophia see at once that his lordship doted on her "to the highest degree of distraction"?

Where the quoted speech is a full sentence requiring a full stop (or other terminal mark) of its own, and coincidentally comes at the end of the containing sentence, the mark inside the inverted commas serves for both:

Then fetching a deep sigh [. . .] he ran on for some minutes in a strain which would be little more pleasing to the reader than it was to the lady; and at last concluded with a declaration, "That if he was master of the world, he would lay it at her feet."

The basic rule is straightforward and logical: when the punctuation relates to the quoted words it goes inside the inverted commas; when it relates to the sentence, it goes outside. Unless, of course, you are in America.

,

So far in this chapter we have looked at punctuation that encourages the reader to inflect words mentally in a straightfor-wardly emphatic way:

Hello!
Hello?
Hello
"Hello"

But, as many classically trained actors will tell you, it can be just as effective to lower your voice for emphasis as to raise it. Poets and writers know this too, which is where dashes and brackets come in. Both of these marks ostensibly muffle your volume and flatten your tone; but, used carefully, they can do more to make a point than any page and a half of italics. Here are some literary dashes:

He learned the arts of riding, fencing, gunnery,
And how to scale a fortress — or a nunnery.
Byron, *Don Juan*, 1818–20

175

Let love therefore be what it will, —
my uncle Toby fell into it.
> Laurence Sterne,
> *Tristram Shandy*, 1760–67

Because I could not stop for Death —
He kindly stopped for me —
The Carriage held but just
    Ourselves —
And Immortality.
> Emily Dickinson, "Because I could
> not stop for Death", 1863

The dash is nowadays seen as the enemy of grammar, partly because overtly disorganised thought is the mode of most email and (mobile phone) text communication, and the dash does an annoyingly good job in these contexts standing in for all other punctuation marks. "I saw Jim — he looked gr8 — have you seen him — what time is the thing 2morrow — C U there." Why is the dash the mark *à la mode?* Because it is so easy to use, perhaps; and because it is hard to use wrongly; but also because it is, simply, easy to *see*. Full stops and commas are often quite tiny in modern typefaces, whereas the handsome horizontal dash is a lot harder to miss. However, just as the exclamation mark used to be *persona non grata* on old typewriter keyboards, so you may often hunt in vain for the dash nowadays: on my own Apple keyboard I have been for years discouraged from any stream-of-consciousness writing by the belief that I had to make my own quasi-dashes from illicit double-taps on the hyphen. When I discovered a week ago that I could make a true dash by employing the alt key with the hyphen, it was truly one of the red-letter days of my life. Meanwhile, the distinction between the big bold dash and its little brother the hyphen is evidently blurring these days, and requires explanation. Whereas a dash is generally concerned to connect (or separate) phrases and sentences, the tiny tricksy hyphen (used above in such phrases as "quasi-dashes", "double-taps" and "stream-of-consciousness") is used quite distinctly to connect (or separate) individual words.

Are dashes intrinsically unserious? Certainly in abundance they suggest baroque and hyperactive silliness, as exemplified by the breathless Miss Bates in Jane Austen's *Emma*:

"How do you do? How do you all do? — Quite well, I am much obliged to you. Never better. —

Don't I hear another carriage? —
Who can this be? — very likely the
worthy Coles. — Upon my word,
this is charming to be standing
about among such friends! And such
a noble fire! — I am quite roasted."

Yet the dash need not be silly. The word
has identical roots with the verb "to dash"
(deriving from the Middle English verb
dasshen, meaning "to knock, to hurl, to
break") and the point is that a single dash
creates a dramatic disjunction which can
be exploited for humour, for bathos, for
shock. "Wait for it," the single dash seems
to whisper, with a twinkle if you're lucky.
Byron is a great master of the dramatic
dash:

> A little still she strove, and much
>   repented,
> And whispering "I will ne'er
>   consent" —
>
>   consented.

A comma just wouldn't cut the mustard
there, especially with the metre hurrying
you along. Meanwhile, Emily Dickinson's
extraordinary penchant for dashes has
been said to be a mirror into her own syn-

apses, symbolising "the analogical leaps and flashes of advanced cognition" — either that, of course, or she used a typewriter from which all the other punctuation keys had been sadistically removed.

Double dashes are another matter. These are a bracketing device, and the only issue is when to use brackets, when dashes. The differences can be quite subtle, but compare these two:

He was (I still can't believe this!) trying to climb in the window.
He was — I still can't believe this! — trying to climb in the window.

Is one version preferable to the other? Reading both aloud, it would be hard to tell them apart. But as they sit on the page, it seems to me that the brackets half-remove the intruding aside, half-suppress it; while the dashes warmly welcome it in, with open arms.

Brackets come in various shapes, types and names:

1 round brackets (which we call brackets, and the Americans call parentheses)

2 square brackets [which we call square brackets, and the Americans call brackets]

3 brace brackets {which are shaped thus and derive from maths}

4 angle brackets < used in palae-ography, linguistics and other technical specialisms >

The angle shape was the earliest to appear, but in the 16th century Erasmus gave the attractive name "lunulae" to round brackets, in reference to their moon-like profile. The word "bracket" — one of the few English punctuation words not to derive from Greek or Latin — comes from the same German root as "brace" and "breeches", and originally referred (deep down you knew this) to the kind of bracket that holds up a bookshelf! The idea that, in writing, brackets lift up a section of a sentence, holding it a foot or two above the rest, is rather satisfying. For the reader, however, the important thing is that this lift-and-hold business doesn't last too long, because there is a certain amount of anxiety created once a bracket has been opened that is not dissipated until it's bloody well closed again. As Oliver Wendell Holmes remarked so beautifully, "One has to dismount from an idea, and get into the saddle again, at every parenthesis." Writers who place whole substantive passages in brackets can't possibly appreciate the existential suffering they inflict. When a bracket opens half-way down a left-hand page and the closing bracket is, giddyingly, nowhere in sight, it's like being in a play by Jean-Paul Sartre.

However, there are plenty of legitimate uses of brackets. First, to add information, to clarify, to explain, to illustrate:

Tom Jones (1749) was considered such a lewd book that, when two earthquakes occurred in London in 1750, Fielding's book was blamed for them.

Starburst (formerly known as Opal Fruits) are available in all corner shops.

Robert Maxwell wasn't dead yet (he was still suing people).

Second, brackets are perfect for authorial asides of various kinds:

The exclamation mark is sometimes called (really!) a dog's cock.

Tom Jones was blamed for some earthquakes (isn't that interesting?).

Square brackets are quite another thing. They are an editor's way of clarifying the meaning of a direct quote without actually changing any of the words:

> She had used it [*Tom Jones*] for quite a number of examples now.

Obviously, the text only says "it" at this point, but the editor needs to be more specific, so inserts the information inside square brackets. It is quite all right to replace the "it", actually:

> She had used [*Tom Jones*] for far too many examples by this stage.

Square brackets are most commonly used around the word *sic* (from the Latin *sicut*, meaning "just as"), to explain the status of an apparent mistake. Generally, *sic* means the foregoing mistake (or apparent mistake) was made by the writer/speaker I am quoting; I am but the faithful messenger; in fact I never get anything wrong myself:

> She asked for "a packet of Starbust [*sic*]".

Book reviewers in particular adore to use *sic*.

It makes them feel terrific, because what it means is that they've spotted this apparent mistake, thank you, so there is no point writing in. However, there are distinctions within *sic*: it can signify two different things:

1 This isn't a mistake, actually; it just looks like one to the casual eye.

> I am grateful to Mrs Bollock [*sic*] for the following examples.

2 Tee hee, what a dreadful error! But it would be dishonest of me to correct it.

> "Please send a copy of *The Time's* [*sic*]," he wrote.

Square brackets also (sometimes) enclose the ellipsis, when words are left out. Thus:

> But a more lucky circumstance happened to poor Sophia: another noise broke forth, which almost drowned her cries [. . .] the door flew open, and in came Squire Western, with his parson, and a set of myrmidons at his heels.

,

I recently heard of someone studying the ellipsis (or three dots) for a PhD. And, I have to say, I was horrified. The ellipsis is the black hole of the punctuation universe, surely, into which no right-minded person would willingly be sucked, for three years, with no guarantee of a job at the end. But at least when this thesis is complete, it may tell us whether rumours are true, and that Mrs Henry Wood's "Dead . . . and never called me mother!" (in the stage version of *East Lynne*) was really the first time it was used. Newspapers sometimes use the ellipsis interchangeably with a dash . . . which can be quite irritating . . . as its proper uses are quite specific, and very few:

1 To indicate words missing . . . from a quoted passage

2 To trail off in an intriguing manner . . .

Which is always a good way to end anything, of course — in an intriguing manner. When you consider the power of erotic suggestion contained in the traditional three-dot chapter ending ("He swept her into his arms. She was powerless to resist. All she knew was, she loved him . . ."), it's a bit of a comedown for the ellipsis to be used as a sub-species of the dash. Perhaps the final word on the ellipsis should go to Peter Cook in this Pete and Dud sketch from BBC2's *Not Only But Also* in 1966. (My memory was that the title of this show contained an ellipsis itself, being *Not Only . . . But Also*, but in modern references the ellipsis has been removed, which only goes to show you can't rely on anything any more.) Anyway, Peter Cook's musing on the significance of the three dots is quite as good a philosophical moment as Tom Stoppard's critics Moon and Birdboot in *The Real Inspector Hound* arguing about whether you can start a play with a pause. Pete is explaining to Dud how a bronzed pilot approaches a woman on a dusty runway in Nevil Shute's *A Town Like Alice* — a woman whose perfectly defined "busty substances" have been outlined underneath her frail poplin dress by a shower of rain and then the "tremendous rushing wind" from his propellers:

DUD: What happened after that, Pete?
PETE: Well, the bronzed pilot goes up
    to her and they walk away, and the
    chapter ends in three dots.

185

DUD: What do those three dots mean, Pete?

PETE: Well, in Shute's hands, three dots can mean anything.

DUD: How's your father, perhaps?

PETE: When Shute uses three dots it means, "Use your own imagination. Conjure the scene up for yourself." (*Pause*) Whenever I see three dots I feel all funny.

A Little Used
Punctuation Mark

One of the most profound things ever said about punctuation came in an old style guide of the Oxford University Press in New York. "If you take hyphens seriously," it said, "you will surely go mad." And it's true. Just look how the little blighter escaped all previous categorisation until I had to hunt it down on its own for this teeny-weeny, hooked-on, afterthought-y chapter. It's a funny old mark, the hyphen. Always has been. People have argued for its abolition for years: Woodrow Wilson said the hyphen was "the most un-American thing in the world" (note the hyphen required in "un-American"); Churchill said hyphens were "a blemish, to be avoided wherever possible". Yet there will always be a problem about getting rid of the hyphen: if it's not extra-marital sex (with a hyphen), it is perhaps extra marital sex, which is quite a different bunch of coconuts. Phrases abound that cry out for hyphens. Those much-invoked examples of the little used car, the superfluous hair remover, the pickled herring merchant, the slow moving traffic and the two hundred odd members of the Conservative Party would all be lost without it.

The name comes from the Greek, as usual. What a lot of words the Greeks had for explaining spatial relationships — for placing round, placing underneath, joining together, cutting off! Lucky for us, otherwise we would have had to call our punctuation marks names like "joiner" and "half a dash" and so on. In this case, the phrase from which we derive the name hyphen means "under one" or "into one" or "together", so is possibly rather more sexy in its origins than we might otherwise have imagined from its utilitarian image today. Traditionally it joins together words, or words-with-prefixes, to aid understanding; it keeps certain other words neatly apart, with an identical intention. Thus the pickled-herring merchant can hold his head high, and the coat-tail doesn't look like an unpronounceable single word. And all thanks to the humble hyphen.

The fate of the hyphen is of course implicated in a general change occurring in the language at the moment, which will be discussed in the next chapter: the astonishing and quite dangerous drift back to the *scriptio continua* of the ancient world, by which words are just hoicked together as "all one word" with no initial capitals or helpful punctuation — the only good result of which being that if books manage to survive more than the next twenty years or so, younger readers will have no trouble reading James Joyce, since unhyphenated poetic compounds like "snotgreen" and "scrotumtightening" will look perfectly everyday. Email addresses are inuring us to this trend, as are advertisements on the internet ("GENTSROLEXWATCH!"), and when I received an invitation to a BBC launch for an initiative called "soundstart", I hardly blinked an eye. In the old days, we used to ask the following question a lot: "One word? Two words? Hyphenated?" With astonishing speed, the third alternative is just disappearing, and I have heard that people with double-barrelled names are simply unable to get the concept across these days, because so few people on the other end of a telephone know what a hyphen is. As a consequence they receive credit cards printed with the name "Anthony Armstrong, Jones", "Anthony Armstrong'Jones", or even "Anthony Armstrong Hyphen".

Where should hyphens still go, before we sink into a depressing world that writes, "Hellohowareyouwhatisthisspacebarthingf oranyidea"? Well, there are many legitimate uses for the hyphen:

1 To prevent people casting aspersions at herring merchants who have never touched a drop in their lives. Many words require hyphens to avoid ambiguity: words such as "co-respondent", "re-formed", "re-mark". A re-formed rock band is quite different from a reformed one. Likewise, a long-standing friend is different from a long standing one. A cross-section of the public is quite different from a cross section of the public. And one could go on. Carefully placed hyphens do not always save the day, however, as I recently had good reason to learn. Writing in *The Daily Telegraph* about the state of modern punctuation, I alluded to a "newspaper style-book" — carefully adding the hyphen to ensure the meaning was clear (I wasn't sure people had heard of style books). And can you believe it? Two people wrote to complain! I had hyphenated wrongly, they said (with glee). Since there was no such thing as a newspaper style-book, I must really have intended "newspaper-style

book". I'll just say here and now that I've rarely been more affronted. "What is a newspaper-style book, then?" I yelled. "Tell me what a newspaper-style book would look like when it's at home!" I still have not got over this.

2 It is still necessary to use hyphens when spelling out numbers, such as thirty-two, forty-nine.

3 When linking nouns with nouns, such as the London-Brighton train; also adjectives with adjectives: American-French relations. Typesetters and publishers use a short dash, known as an en-rule, for this function.

4 Though it is less rigorously applied than it used to be, there is a rule that when a noun phrase such as "stainless steel" is used to qualify another noun, it is hyphenated, as "stainless-steel kitchen". Thus you have corrugated iron, but a corrugated-iron roof. The match has a second half, but lots of second-half excitement. *Tom Jones* was written in the 18th century, but is an 18th-century novel. The train leaves at seven o'clock; it is the seven-o'clock train.

5 Certain prefixes traditionally require hyphens: un-American, anti-Apartheid, pro-hyphens, quasi-grammatical.

6 When certain words are to be spelled out, it is customary to use hyphens to indicate that you want the letters enunciated (or pictured) separately: "K-E-Y-N-S-H-A-M".

7 Purely for expediency, the hyphen is used to avoid an unpleasant linguistic condition called "letter collision". However much you might want to create compound words, there will always be some ghastly results, such as "deice" (de-ice) or "shelllike" (shell-like).

8 One of the main uses of the hyphen, of course, is to indicate that a word is unfinished and continues on the next line. Ignorance about where to split words has reached quite scary proportions, but thankfully this isn't the place to go into it. I'll just say that it's "pains-]taking" and not "pain-]staking".

9 Hesitation and stammering are indicated by hyphens: "I reached for the w-w-w-watering can."

10 When a hyphenated phrase is coming up, and you are qualifying it beforehand, it is necessary to write, "He was a two- or three-year-old."

Even bearing all these rules in mind, however, one can't help feeling that the hyphen is for the chop. Fowler's *Modern English Usage* as far back as 1930 was advising that, "wherever reasonable", the hyphen should be dropped, and the 2003 edition of the *Oxford Dictionary of English* suggests that it is heading for extinction. American usage is gung-ho for compound words (or should that be gungho?), but a state of confusion reigns these days, with quite psychotic hyphenations arising in British usage, especially the rise of hyphens in phrasal verbs. "Time to top-up that pension," the advertisements tell us. Uneducated football writers will aver that the game "kicked-off" at 3pm, and are not, apparently, ticked off afterwards. On the *Times* books website I see that Joan Smith "rounds-up" the latest crime fiction. But what if a writer wants his hyphens and can make a case for them? Nicholson Baker in his book *The Size of Thoughts* writes about his own deliberations when a well-intentioned copy-editor deleted about two hundred "innocent tinkertoy hyphens" in the manuscript of one of his books. American copy-editing, he says, has fallen into a state of "demoralised confusion" over hyphenated and unhyphenated compounds. On this occasion he wrote "stet hyphen" (let the hyphen stand) so many times in the margin that, in the end, he abbreviated it to "SH".

> I stetted myself sick over the new manuscript. I stetted *re-enter* (rather than *reenter*), *post-doc* (rather than *postdoc*), *foot-pedal* (rather than *foot pedal*), *second-hand* (rather than *second-hand*), *twist-tie* (rather than *twist tie*), and *pleasure-nubbins* (rather than *pleasure nubbins*).

It is probably better not to inquire what "pleasure-nubbins" refers to here, incidentally, while still defending Baker's right to hyphenate his pleasure-nubbins — yes, even all day, if he wants to.

In the end, hyphen usage is just a big bloody mess and is likely to get messier. When you consider that fifty years ago it was correct to hyphenate Oxford Street as "Oxford-street", or "tomorrow" as "tomorrow", you can't help feeling that prayer for eventual light-in-our-darkness may be the only sane course of action. Interestingly, Kingsley Amis says that those who smugly object to the hyphenation of the phrase "fine tooth-comb" are quite wrong to assert the phrase ought really to be punctuated "fine-tooth comb". Evidently there really used to be a kind of comb called a tooth-comb, and you could buy it in varieties of fineness. Isn't it a relief to know that? You learn something new every day.

Merely Conventional Signs

On page 33 of the first-edition copy of Eric Partridge's *You Have a Point There* that I have before me as I write (I borrowed it from the University of London Library), there is a marginal note made by a reader long ago. A marginal note? Yes, and I have been back to check and muse on it several times. Partridge, who is just about to elucidate the 17th application of the comma ("Commas in Fully Developed Complex Sentences"), is explaining that in this particular case it is difficult to formulate a set of rigid rules. "My aim is to be helpful, not dogmatic," he explains. "The following examples will, if examined and pondered, supply the data from which any person of average intelligence can, without strain, assimilate an unformulated set of working rules." At which the unknown, long-ago reader has written in old-fashioned handwriting up the side, "Rot! You lazy swine Partridge."

There are two reasons why I have borne this ballpoint outburst in mind while writing this book. One is that if *Eric Par-*

tridge wasn't comprehensive enough for some people, there is obviously naff-all chance for me. But there is also the fact that this startling effusion has lain within the pages of *You Have a Point There* possibly for fifty years, which is as long as the book itself has been a book. And this makes me wistful. The future of books is a large subject and perhaps this is not a suitable place to pursue it. We hear every day that the book is dead and that even the dimmest child can find "anything" on the internet. Yet I'm afraid I have to stick my small oar in because — as I hope has become clear from the foregoing chapters — our system of punctuation was produced in the age of printing, by printers, and is reliant on the ascendancy of printing to survive. Our punctuation exists as a printed set of conventions; it has evolved slowly because of printing's innate conservatism; and is effective only if readers have been trained to appreciate the nuances of the printed page. The good news for punctuation is that the age of printing has been glorious and has held sway for more than half a millennium. The bad news for punctuation, however, is that the age of printing is due to hold its official retirement party next Friday afternoon at half-past five.

"I blame all the emails and text messages," people say, when you talk about the decline in punctuation standards. Well, *yes*. The effect on language of the electronic age is obvious to all, even though the process has only just begun, and its ultimate impact is as yet unimaginable.

"I write quite differently in emails," people say, with a look of inspired and happy puzzlement — a look formerly associated only with starry-eyed returnees from alien abduction. "Yes, I write quite differently in emails, especially in the punctuation. I feel it's OK to use dashes all the time, and exclamation marks. And those dot, dot, dot things!"

"Ellipsis," I interject.

"I can't seem to help it!" they continue. "It's as if I've never heard of semicolons! Dot, dot, dot! And everyone's doing the same!"

This is an exciting time for the written word: it is adapting to the ascendant medium, which happens to be the most immediate, universal and democratic written medium that has ever existed. But it is all happening too quickly for some people, and we have to face some uncomfortable facts: for example, it is already too late to campaign for Heinz to add punctuation marks to the Alphabetti Spaghetti, in the hope that all will be well.

Having grown up as readers of the printed word (and possibly even scribblers in margins), we may take for granted the processes involved in the traditional activity of reading — so let us remind ourselves. The printed word is presented to us in a linear way, with syntax supreme in conveying the sense of the words in their order. We read privately, mentally listening to the writer's voice and translating the writer's thoughts. The book remains static and fixed; the reader journeys through it. Picking up the book in the first place entails an active pursuit of understanding. Holding the book, we are aware of posterity and continuity. Knowing that the printed word is always edited, typeset and proof-read before it reaches us, we appreciate its literary authority. Having paid money for it (often), we have a sense of investment and a pride of ownership, not to mention a feeling of general virtue.

All these conditions for reading are overturned by the new technologies. Information is presented to us in a non-linear way, through an exponential series of lateral associations. The internet is a public "space" which you visit, and even inhabit; its product is inherently impersonal and dis-embodied. Scrolling documents is the op-posite of reading: your eyes remain static, while the material flows past. Despite all the opportunities to "interact", we read material from the internet (or CD-roms, or whatever) entirely passively because all the interesting associative thinking has already been done on our behalf. Electronic media are intrinsically ephemeral, are open to perpetual revision, and work quite strenu-ously against any sort of historical percep-tion. The opposite of edited, the material on the internet is unmediated, except by the technology itself. And having no price, it has questionable value. Finally, you can't write comments in the margin of your screen to be discovered by another reader fifty years down the line.

Having said all this, there is no imme-diate cause for panic. If the book is dying, then at least it is treating its loyal fans (and the bookshops) to an extravagant and ex-tended swan song. But when we look around us at the state of literacy — and in particular at all those signs for "BOBS' MOTORS" and "ANTIQUE,S" — it just has to be borne in mind that books are no longer the main vehicles for language in modern society, and that if our fate is in the hands of the barbarians, there is an observable cultural drift that can only make matters worse. As I mentioned in this book's introduction, by tragic historical coincidence a period of abysmal under-educating in literacy has coincided with this unexpected explosion of global self-publishing. Thus people who don't know their apostrophe from their elbow are positively invited to disseminate their writings to anyone on the planet stupid enough to double-click and scroll. Mark Twain said it many years ago, but it has never been more true:

> There is no such thing as "the Queen's English". The property has gone into the hands of a joint stock company and we own the bulk of the shares!
> *Following the Equator,* 1897

'

It hurts, though. It hurts like hell. Even in the knowledge that our punctuation has arrived at its present state by a series of accidents; even in the knowledge that there are at least seventeen rules for the comma, some of which are beyond explanation by top grammarians — it is a matter for despair to see punctuation chucked out as worthless by people who don't know the difference between *who's* and *whose,* and whose bloody automatic "grammar checker" can't tell the difference either. And despair was the initial impetus for this book. I saw a sign for "Book's" with an apostrophe in it, and something deep inside me snapped; snapped with that melancholy sound you hear in Chekhov's *The Cherry Orchard,* like a far-off cable breaking in a mine-shaft. I know that language moves on. It has to. Not once have I ever stopped to feel sorry for those Egyptian hieroglyph artists tossed on the scrapheap during a former linguistic transition ("Birds' heads in profile, mate? You having a laugh?"). But I can't help feeling that our punctuation system, which has served the written word with grace and ingenuity for centuries, must not be allowed to disappear without a fight.

Nothing as scary as this has confronted punctuation before. True, Gertrude Stein banged on a bit. But attacks on punctuation have always been feeble. The Futurists of the early 20th century had a go, but without much lasting effect. In 1913, F. T. Marinetti wrote a manifesto he called *Destruction of Syntax/Imagination without Strings/Words-in-Freedom* which demanded the moral right of words to live unfettered — and only slightly undermined its case by requiring such a lot of punctuation in the title.

> By the imagination without strings [wrote Marinetti] I mean the absolute freedom of images or analogies, or expressed with unhampered words and with no connecting strings of syntax and with no punctuation.

Marinetti wanted to explode the "so-called typographical harmony of the page" and he was influential both on poetry and on graphic design. Reading him now, however, one's main impression is of a rather weedy visionary who fell asleep one night, saw in a dream how to use QuarkXPress, and was then cruelly deposited back again in the days before the First World War.

> On the same page, therefore, we will use three or four colours of ink, or even twenty different typefaces if necessary. For example: italics for a series of swift sensations, boldface for violent onomatopoeias, and so on. With this typographical revolution and this multi-coloured variety in the letters I mean to

redouble the expressive force of words.

So much for Marinetti, then. Meanwhile, George Bernard Shaw, along with his famous doomed campaign to reform the spelling of the English language, had already started making efforts to undermine the contractive apostrophe. And while he certainly had more global influence than Marinetti did, he remained a one-man campaign. It is a measure of Shaw's considerable monomania, by the way, that in 1945 he wrote to *The Times* on the issue of the recently deployed atomic bomb to point out that since the second "b" in the word bomb was needless (I'm not joking), enormous numbers of working hours were being lost to the world through the practice of conforming to traditional spelling.

I can scribble the word "bomb" barely legibly 18 times in one minute and "bom" 24 times, saving 25 per cent per minute by dropping the superfluous b. In the British Commonwealth, on which the sun never sets, and in the United States of North America, there are always millions of people continually writing, writing, writing . . . Those who are writing are losing time at the rate of $131,400 \times x$ per annum . . .

Abraham Tauber (ed.),
George Bernard Shaw on Language, 1965

Yes, GBS can be a pretty stark reminder of how far one may lose one's sense of proportion when obsessed by matters of language.

But on the other hand he still writes better about language than most people, and in *The Author* in April 1902 he set out his "Notes on the Clarendon Press Rules for Compositors and Readers", which included not only a brilliant attack on those "uncouth bacilli" (apostrophes) which appear so unnecessarily in words such as "dont" and "shant", but was rather wonderful on italics too, and is perhaps where *The Guardian* got its ideas from:

Not only should titles not be printed in italic; but the customary ugly and unnecessary inverted commas should be abolished. Let me give a specimen. 1. I was reading The Merchant of Venice. 2. I was reading "The Merchant of Venice." 3. I was reading *The Merchant of Venice*. The man who cannot see that

No. 1 is the best looking as well as the sufficient and sensible form, should print or write nothing but advertisements for lost dogs or ironmongers' catalogues: literature is not for him to meddle with.

Note the way Shaw (or his editor) puts the full stop inside the inverted commas in example two, by the way. While individual obsessives seem to have made little impact on the development of punctuation in the 20th century (Shaw had few followers, and nobody remembers the Futurists), it is quite clear that punctuation did develop quite robustly under other kinds of cultural pressure. Hyphenation practice has changed hugely in the past hundred years; also capitalisation, and the presentation of all forms of address. Nowadays we write:

Andrew Franklin
Profile Books
58A Hatton Garden
London EC1N 8LX

Or, let's face it, *I* write that because he's my publisher. But my point is: there is no punctuation in this at all, whereas just twenty years ago I would have written:

Mr. A. Franklin, Esq.,
Profile Books, Ltd.,
58A, Hatton Garden,
London, E.C.1

Those of us who were taught to place full stops after abbreviations have simply adapted to a world in which they are not required. I don't write *pub.* or *'bus,* but I'm quite sure I used to. When I trained as a journalist twenty-five years ago, the intermediate rule on matters of address was that if the contraction of a title still ended with the original final letter — thus "Mr" for "Mister", or "Fr" for "Father" — no full stop was required, whereas if the title was cut short — "Prof" for "Professor" or "M" for "Monsieur" — a full stop was essential. I doubt anyone bothers with that distinction any more. It is worth pointing out, though, that American usage has retained a lot of the formal niceties that we have dropped. They also often use a colon after "Dear Andrew", while on this side of the Atlantic we dither about whether even a comma looks a bit fussy.

There are other large changes to punctuation practice in our own lifetimes that have not troubled us much. Nobody says, "You can find it at BBC full stop Co full stop UK," do they? Even the most hide-bound of us don't mind this word "dot" getting into the language. Above all, though, a revolution in typographical spacing occurred so quietly that very few people noticed. Spaces were closed up; other spaces were opened; nobody campaigned. Dashes which were once of differing lengths for different occasions are now generally shorter, of uniform length, and sit between spaces. Until very recently, typists were taught to leave a two- or even three-space gap after a full stop, but now word-processing programs will automatically reduce the gap to a single word space. Semicolons and colons used to have a word space preceding them, and two spaces after, and to be honest, it looked very elegant : but nobody does that any more.

My point is that while massive change from the printed word to the bloody electronic signal is inevitably upon us, we die-hard punctuation-lovers are perhaps not as rigid as we think we are. And we must guard against over-reacting. Those who identify "Netspeak" with *Nineteen Eighty-Four*'s "Newspeak" (on the basis that non-case-sensitive compound words such as "thoughtcrime" and "doubleplusgood" bear a superficial resemblance to "chat-room" and "newsgroup") should urgently reconsider this association, not least because the key virtues of the internet are that it is not controlled by anyone, cannot be used as an instrument of oppression and is endlessly inclusive: its embracing of multitudes even extends to chatrooms in which, believe it or not, are discussed matters of punctuation. A site called "half-bakery", for example, encourages correspondents with attractive names such as "gizmo" and "cheeselikesubstance" to swap ideas about punctuation reform. This is where the intriguing idea of using a tilde to sort out tricky plurals such as "bananas" came from. In one rather thrilling exchange in 2001, moreover, a member of the halfbakery crowd proposed the use of the upside-down question mark (¿) as a marker for a rhetorical question. This suggestion hung there like a bat in a cave for eighteen months until, astonishingly, someone called "Drifting Snowflake" wrote in to explain that a rhetorical question mark (the reversed one) existed already, "invented in the 16th century, though only in use for about 30 years". Gosh. I wonder if Drifting Snowflake is male and unmarried? As the internet is dedicated to proving, you really have no idea who anybody is out there.

What to call the language generated by this new form of communication? Netspeak? Weblish? Whatever you call it, linguists are generally excited by it. Naomi Baron has called Netspeak an "emerging language centaur — part speech, part writing" and David Crystal says computer-mediated language is a genuine "third medium". But I don't know. Remember that thing Truman Capote said years ago about Jack Kerouac: "That's not writing, it's typing"? I keep thinking that what we do now, with this medium of instant delivery, isn't writing, and doesn't even qualify as typing either: it's just sending. What did you do today? Sent a lot of stuff. "Don't forget to send, dear." Receiving, sending and arithmetic — we can say goodbye to the three R's, clearly. Where valuable office hours used to be lost to people schmoozing at the water cooler, they are now sacrificed to people publishing second-hand jokes to every person in their email address book. We send pictures, videos, web addresses, homilies, petitions and (of course) hoax virus alerts, which we later have to apologise for. The medium and the message have never been so strongly identified. As for our writing personally to each other, how often do you hear people complain that emails subtract the tone of voice; that it's hard to tell if someone is joking or not? Clicking on "send" has its limitations as a system of subtle communication. Which is why, of course, people use so many dashes and italics and capitals ("I AM joking!") to compensate. That's why they came up with the emoticon, too — the emoticon being the greatest (or most desperate, depending how you look at it) advance in punctuation since the question mark in the reign of Charlemagne.

You will know all about emoticons. Emoticons are the proper name for smileys. And a smiley is, famously, this:

: —)

Forget the idea of selecting the right words in the right order and channelling the reader's attention by means of artful pointing. Just add the right emoticon to your email and everyone will know what self-expressive effect you thought you kind-of had in mind. Anyone interested in punctuation has a dual reason to feel aggrieved about smileys, because not only are they a paltry substitute for expressing oneself properly; they are also designed by people who evidently thought the punctuation marks on the standard keyboard cried out for an ornamental function. What's this dot-on-top-of-a-dot thing for? What earthly good is it? Well, if you look at it sideways, it could be a pair of eyes. What's this curvy thing for? It's a mouth, look! Hey, I think we're on to something.

: — (

Now it's sad!

; —)

It looks like it's winking!

: — r

It looks like it's sticking its tongue out! The permutations may be endless:

: ˜/ mixed up!
<: —) dunce!
: — [pouting!
: —O surprise!

Well, that's enough. I've just spotted a third reason to loathe emoticons, which is that when they pass from fashion (and I do hope they already have), future generations will associate punctuation marks with an outmoded and rather primitive graphic pastime and despise them all the more. "Why do they still have all these keys with things like dots and spots and eyes and mouths and things?" they will grumble. "*Nobody* does smileys any more."

,

Where does this leave people who love the comma and apostrophe? Where can we turn for consolation? Well, it is useful to remember how depressing the forecasts for language used to be, before the internet came along. Thirty years ago we assumed that television was the ultimate enemy of literacy and that, under the onslaught from image and sound, the written word would rapidly die out. Such fears, at least, have been dissipated. With text messaging and emailing becoming such compulsive universal activities, reading and writing are now more a fact of everyday life than they have ever been. The text message may be a vehicle for some worrying verbal shorthand ("CU B4 8?"), yet every time a mobile goes "Beep-beep; beep-beep" annoyingly within earshot on the bus, we should be grateful for a technological miracle that stepped in unexpectedly to save us from a predicted future that couldn't read at all. As David Crystal writes in his book *Language and the Internet* (2001), the internet encourages a playful and creative (and continuing) relationship with the written word. "The human linguistic faculty seems to be in good shape," he concludes. "The arrival of Netspeak is showing us *homo loquens* at its best."

Punctuation as we know it, however, is surely in for a rocky time. Before the advent of the internet, our punctuation system was very conservative about admitting new marks; indeed, it held out for decades while a newfangled and rather daft symbol called the "interrobang" (invented in 1962) tried to infiltrate the system, disguised as a question mark on top of an exclamation. The idea was that, when you said, "Where did you get that hat?!" you needed an interrobang to underline the full expression, and it is delightful to note that absolutely nobody was interested in giving it house-room. But I'm sure they will now, once they find out. Anything new is welcome today. People experiment with asterisks to show emphasis ("What a *day* I've had!") and also angle brackets ("So have

< I > !"). Yes, the interrobang will find its place at last — especially given that its name has overtones of a police interview terminating in an explosion. Violent path-lab terminology is very much in vogue in the modern world of punctuation. Remember when we used to call the solidus (/) a "stroke"?

"Yes, you can see the bullet points here, here and here, sir; there are multiple back-slashes, of course. And that's a forward slash. I would have to call this a frenzied attack. Did anyone hear the interrobang?"

"Oh yes. Woman next door was temporarily deafened by it. What's this?"

"Ah. You don't see many of these any more. It's an emoticon. Hold your head this way and it appears to be winking."

"Good God! You mean — ?"

"That's the mouth."

"You mean — ?"

"That's the nose."

"Good grief. Then it's — ?"

"Oh yes, sir. There's no doubt about it, sir. The Punctuation Murderer has struck again."

Is it an option to cling on to the punctuation and grammar we know and love? Hope occasionally flares up and dies down again. In May 1999, Bob Hirschfield wrote a news story in *The Washington Post* about a computer virus "far more insidious than the recent Chernobyl menace" that was spreading throughout the internet. What did this virus do? Named the Strunkenwhite Virus (after *The Elements of Style* by William Strunk and E. B. White, a classic American style guide), it refused to deliver emails containing grammatical mistakes. Could it be true? Was the world to be saved at a stroke (or even, if we must, at a forward slash)? Sadly, no. The story was a wind-up. Hirschfield's intention in inventing the Strunkenwhite Virus for the delight of his readers was simply to satirise the public's appetite for wildly improbable virus scare stories. In the process, however, he painted such a heavenly vision of future grammatical happiness that he inadvertently broke the hearts of sticklers everywhere:

The virus is causing something akin to panic throughout corporate America, which has become used to the typos, misspellings, missing words and mangled syntax so acceptable in cyberspace. The

CEO of LoseItAll.com, an Internet startup, said the virus had rendered him helpless. "Each time I tried to send one particular e-mail this morning, I got back this error message: 'Your dependent clause preceding your independent clause must be set off by commas, but one must not precede the conjunction.' I threw my laptop across the room."

. . . If Strunkenwhite makes e-mailing impossible, it could mean the end to a communication revolution once hailed as a significant timesaver. A study of 1,254 office workers in Leonia, N.J., found that e-mail increased employees' productivity by 1.8 hours a day because they took less time to formulate their thoughts. (The same study also found that they lost 2.2 hours of productivity because they were e-mailing so many jokes to their spouses, parents and stockbrokers.)

. . . "This is one of the most complex and invasive examples of computer code we have ever encountered. We just can't imagine what kind of devious mind would want to tamper with e-mails to create this burden on communications," said an FBI agent who insisted on speaking via the telephone out of concern that trying to e-mail his comments could leave him tied up for hours.

Hirschfield's story ended with the saddest invention of all:

Meanwhile bookstores and online booksellers reported a surge in orders for Strunk & White's "The Elements of Style."

,

Given all that we know about the huge changes operating on our language at the moment — and given all that we know about the shortcomings of the punctuation system produced by the age of printing — should we be bothering to fight for the 17 uses of the comma, or the appositive colon? Isn't it the case, in the end, that punctuation is just a set of conventions, and that conventions have no intrinsic worth? One can't help remembering the moment in Lewis Carroll's *The Hunting of the Snark* when the Bellman exhibits his blank map and asks the crew how they feel about it:

"What use are Mercator's North Poles and Equators,

Tropics, Zones and Meridian Lines?"
So the Bellman would cry: and the
  crew would reply,
"They are merely conventional signs!"
          Lewis Carroll,
          The Hunting of the Snark, 1876

But after journeying through the world of punctuation, and seeing what it can do, I am all the more convinced we should fight like tigers to preserve our punctuation, and we should start now. Who wants a blank map, for heaven's sake? There is more at stake than the way people read and write. Note the way the *Washington Post* news story explained the benefits of emailing: it "increased employees' productivity by 1.8 hours a day *because they took less time to formulate their thoughts*". If we value the way we have been trained to think by centuries of absorbing the culture of the printed word, we must not allow the language to return to the chaotic *scriptio continua* swamp from which it so bravely crawled less than two thousand years ago. We have a language that is full of ambiguities; we have a way of expressing ourselves that is often complex and allusive, poetic and modulated; all our thoughts can be rendered with absolute clarity if we bother to put the right dots and squiggles between the words in the right places. Proper punctuation is both the sign and the cause of clear thinking. If it goes, the degree of intellectual impoverishment we face is unimaginable.

One of the best descriptions of punctuation comes in a book entitled *The Fiction Editor, the Novel, and the Novelist* (1989) by Thomas McCormack. He says the purpose of punctuation is "to tango the reader into the pauses, inflections, continuities and connections that the spoken line would convey":

> Punctuation to the writer is like anatomy to the artist: He learns the rules so he can knowledgeably and controllédly depart from them as art requires. Punctuation is a means, and its end is: helping the reader to hear, to follow.

And here's a funny thing. If all these high moral arguments have had no effect, just remember that ignorance of punctuation can have rather large practical repercussions in the real world. In February 2003 a Cambridge politics lecturer named Glen Rangwala received a copy of the

British government's most recent dossier on Iraq. He quickly recognised in it the wholesale copying of a twelve-year-old thesis by American doctoral student Ibrahim al-Marashi, "reproduced word for word, misplaced comma for misplaced comma". Oh yes. Rangwala noticed there were some changes to the original, such as the word "terrorists" substituted for "opposition groups", but otherwise much of it was identical. In publishing his findings, he wrote:

> Even the typographical errors and anomalous uses of grammar are incorporated into the Downing Street document. For example, Marashi had written:
> "Saddam appointed, Sabir 'Abd al-'Aziz al-Duri as head" . . .
> Note the misplaced comma. The UK officials who used Marashi's text hadn't. Thus, on page 13, the British dossier incorporates the same misplaced comma:
> "Saddam appointed, Sabir 'Abd al-'Aziz al-Duri as head" . . .

So we ignore the rules of punctuation at our political peril as well as to our moral detriment. When Sir Roger Casement was "hanged on a comma" all those years ago, who would have thought a British government would be rumbled on a comma (and a "yob's comma", at that) ninety years further down the line? Doesn't it feel good to know this, though? It does. It really does.

Bibliography

Robert Allen, *Punctuation*, Oxford University Press, 2002

Kingsley Amis, *The King's English: a guide to modern usage*, HarperCollins, 1997

Anon, *A Treatise of Stops, Points, or Pauses, and of notes which are used in Writing and Print*, 1680

Tim Austin, *The Times Guide to English Style and Usage*, Times Books, 1999

Nicholson Baker, "The History of Punctuation", in *The Size of Thoughts*, Chatto & Windus, 1996

— *Room Temperature*, Granta Books, 1990

Sven Birkerts, *The Gutenberg Elegies: the fate of reading in an electronic age*, Ballantine, 1994

Bill Bryson, *Mother Tongue: the English language*, Hamish Hamilton, 1990

— *Troublesome Words*, third edition, Viking, 2001

R. W. Burchfield, *The New Fowler's Modern English Usage*, revised third edition, Oxford University Press, 1998

Rene J. Cappon, *The Associated Press Guide to Punctuation*, Perseus Publishing, 2003

G. V. Carey, *Mind the Stop: a brief guide to punctuation with a note on proof-correction*, Cambridge University Press, 1939

— *Punctuation*, Cambridge University Press, 1957

David Crystal, *Cambridge Encyclopedia of the English Language*, Cambridge University Press, 1995

— *Language and the Internet*, Cambridge University Press, 2001

Kay Cullen (ed.), *Chambers Guide to Punctuation*, Chambers, 1999

H. W. Fowler, *The King's English*, Clarendon Press, Oxford University Press, 1906

Karen Elizabeth Gordon, *The New Well-Tempered Sentence: a punctuation handbook for the innocent, the eager, and the doomed*, Houghton Mifflin, 1993

Ernest Gowers, *Plain Words: a guide to the use of English*, HMSO, 1948

Cecil Hartley, *Principles of Punctuation: or, The Art of Pointing*, 1818

Philip Howard, *The State of the Language: English observed*, Hamish Hamilton, 1984

F. T. Husband and M. F. A. Husband, *Punctuation, its Principles and Practice*, Routledge, 1905

Ben Jonson, *English Grammar*, 1640

Graham King, *Punctuation*, HarperCollins, 2000

Thomas McCormack, *The Fiction Editor, the Novel, and the Novelist*, Sidgwick & Jackson, 1989

John McDermott, *Punctuation for Now*, Macmillan, 1990

Malcolm Parkes, *Pause and Effect: an introduction to the history of punctuation in the West*, Scolar Press, 1992

Eric Partridge, *Usage and Abusage: a guide to good English*, Hamish Hamilton, 1947

— *You Have a Point There*, Hamish Hamilton, 1953

Joseph Robertson, *An Essay on Punctuation*, 1785

Paul A. Robinson, "The Philosophy of Punctuation", in *Opera, Sex, and Other Vital Matters*, Chicago University Press, 2002

Paul Saenger, *Space between Words: the origins of silent reading*, Stanford University Press, 1997

Reginald Skelton, *Modern English Punctuation*, Pitman, 1933

Gertrude Stein, "Poetry and Grammar", in *Look at Me Now and Here I Am: writings and lectures 1911–45*, Peter Owen, 1967 (reissue imminent)

William Strunk and E. B. White, *The Elements of Style*, fourth edition, Longman, 2000

Abraham Tauber (ed.), *George Bernard Shaw on Language*, Peter Owen, 1965

James Thurber, *The Years with Ross*, Hamish Hamilton, 1959

James Thurber (eds. Helen Thurber and Edward Weeks), *Selected Letters of James Thurber*, Hamish Hamilton, 1982

Loreto Todd, *Cassell's Guide to Punctuation*, Cassell & Co., 1995

R. L. Trask, *The Penguin Guide to Punctuation*, Penguin, 1997

William Vandyck, *Punctuation Repair Kit*, Hodder Headline, 1996

Bill Walsh, *Lapsing into a Comma: a curmudgeon's guide to the many things that can go wrong in print — and how to avoid them*, Contemporary Books, 2000

Keith Waterhouse, *English Our English (and How to Sing It)*, Viking, 1991

— *Sharon & Tracy & the Rest: the best of Keith Waterhouse in the Daily Mail*,

Hodder & Stoughton, 1992

— *Waterhouse on Newspaper Style*, Viking, 1989

About the Author

Lynne Truss is a writer and journalist who started out as a literary editor with a blue pencil and then got sidetracked. The author of three novels and numerous radio comedy dramas, she spent six years as the television critic of _The Times_ (London), followed by four (rather peculiar) years as a sports columnist for the same newspaper. She won Columnist of the Year for her work for _Women's Journal._ She now reviews books for _The Sunday Times_ (London) and is a familiar voice on BBC Radio 4. She lives in Brighton, England.

www.eatsshootsandleaves.com